THE NATION'S
FAVOURITE
TWENTIETH CENTURY POEMS

The 10 most popular poems from the 1996 poll
to find the nation's favourite modern poem.

1. Warning
JENNY JOSEPH

2. Not Waving but Drowning
STEVIE SMITH

3. Do not go gentle into that good night
DYLAN THOMAS

4. This Be the Verse
PHILIP LARKIN

5. Stop all the clocks
W.H. AUDEN

6. The Whitsun Weddings
PHILIP LARKIN

7. Fern Hill
DYLAN THOMAS

8. If—
RUDYARD KIPLING

9. Christmas
SIR JOHN BETJEMAN

10. Diary of a Church Mouse
SIR JOHN BETJEMAN

*

THE NATION'S FAVOURITE TWENTIETH CENTURY POEMS

— ◇ —

EDITED BY

GRIFF RHYS JONES

Published by
BBC Worldwide Limited,
Woodlands,
80 Wood Lane,
London
W12 0TT

First published 1999
Compilation © Griff Rhys Jones 1999
Poems © individual copyright holders

ISBN: 0 563 55143 7

Set in Stempel Garamond by Keystroke,
Jacaranda Lodge, Wolverhampton.
Printed and bound in Great Britain by Martins the Printers Ltd,
Berwick-upon-Tweed.
Cover printed by Belmont Press, Northampton.

CONTENTS

— ◇ —

– Contents –

'. . . we have no hope of better
Happiness than this, . . . '

'In labour-saving homes, with care
Their wives frizz out peroxide hair'

'For human beings only do
What their religion tells them to'

– Contents –

'Between the streams and the red clouds, hearing curlews'

'I believe life ends with death, and that is all'

'For there is good news yet to hear and fine things to be seen'

'Time held me green and dying'

'Things fall apart; the centre cannot hold;
Mere anarchy is loosed upon the world'

– Contents –

FOREWORD BY GRIFF RHYS JONES

— ◇ —

Here is another selection of first-rate poetry: comic, moving, pertinent, witty, sharp, short and longish. Gathered together in this book is a comprehensive selection of the finest verse of the last hundred years. A host of different voices, which I hope will surprise and entertain in their variety and scope. Modern poetry is not the difficult and inaccessible stuff that popular imagination would have it. These poems really mean something to a lot of people.

Well, there we are. I can write with such breezy confidence because this selection is actually new and surprising to me as well, though not everybody seems to understand this. After the success of *The Nation's Favourite Poems*, for instance, a doctor from Persia sent me a poem of his own. There was a note with it: 'I hope you will agree with the many who have told me that this is the best poem ever written in the sonnet form and include it in your next anthology.'

Alas for the doctor, the retired coal miner, the former redcoat, and the many other aspiring poets who send me their work, the judgement as to whether they have written the best, or possibly the worst, poetry in the English language does not rest with me. The poems included in this volume, as in the other books in this series, were all voted for by 'the nation' in a television poll. While a significant proportion of the nation may have overlooked their duty in this respect, the number of people who do bother to vote is actually quite large. Large enough to pre-empt block claques and family conspiracies anyway.

The hundred or so poems promoted here are largely familiar works from acknowledged writers. Even the exciting sounding 'The Nightmare' by W.H. Auden turned out on closer enquiry to be the rather more familiar poem, 'Night Mail'. We have also had to re-include some favourites from that classic of the genre, *The Nation's Favourite Poems* (which was open to contenders from the entire span of human creativity).

Nonetheless, bizarrely, the nation's favourite poem of all time, Kipling's 'If—', is not the nation's favourite modern poem of the last hundred years. Perhaps some of the nation is unaware that it was

11

written in 1912. (This may be the same section of the nation who voted for Wordsworth's 'The Daffodils' and Christina Rossetti's 'Remember'.) But then, everybody knows that 'modern poetry' is different from 'poetry'. It does not rhyme or scan and tends to deal with difficult subjects, except, er, here.

Philip Larkin identified the quality of a good poem as being the capturing of a specific emotional moment. Certainly choosing your absolute single favourite poem of the last hundred years is a demanding choice and it comes as no surprise that this selection tends towards the lyrical. Here are poems which people have stored away for later use, which encapsulate feeling rather than analysis. It is not that the experiments of modern poetry have been entirely ignored: there were votes for T.S. Eliot (in reflective mood) for example. But most of the great movements and significant advances seem to have failed to lodge in the heart. No Imagists, no Concrete, no Ezra Pound, no Thom Gunn. Favourite poems seem more likely to be emotional rather than intellectual. Those sometimes-despised sentimental Georgian poets will not lie down.

If, in some circles, the twentieth century is notable mainly for breaking ground and moulds and daring innovation, the nation itself seems wholly unconvinced. Most of the poetry here would be recognisable to Palgrave. There were times, as the votes were counted, when this book threatened to be the *Collected Works of Sir John Betjeman*. He along with Philip Larkin, Ted Hughes, Dylan Thomas and Seamus Heaney jostle for top position as favourite modern poet.

W.H. Auden is well represented too, but in his less 'coded' work. (His film work, in fact. 'Night Mail' was the commentary for a documentary, and 'Stop all the clocks' became famous, of course, thanks to *Four Weddings and a Funeral*.) Our electorate seems to like a simple approach to a complex matter. I was once on a literary committee where several members vigorously attacked the distinguished Welsh poet R.S. Thomas for his 'clichés', by which they meant, possibly, the familiarity of his subjects and images: fields, farming, the burdens of life and so forth. But perhaps the poetry that people love and revere, ancient or modern, has always addressed itself to those familiar subjects rather better than any other literary form, and will always continue to do so.

Setting aside the appreciation of nature, there is an awful lot of loss here. Deaths of fathers figure strongly, and deaths of children and spouses too. And, of course, the contemplation of his or her own death is never far from the true poet's mind. Birth is also celebrated; though with a certain poetic foreboding, and usually with allusions to the infant's ultimate death.

For relief from births and deaths, you can turn to poems by Robert Graves, or Dylan Thomas. There are so many modern funny poets that it seems a pity there are not more here. Perhaps wry and detached irony does not a favourite make. Except in the case of the winning poem, of course. It was a shock to many, including, so I was told, the author, Jenny Joseph, that 'Warning' romped home ahead of the field. The producer had to go and look it up. (So did I, but it was the producer's job.) Some have said that the choice had something to do with the fact that the poem has been prominently featured on a best-selling tea towel. I find books easier to take on a train, but I have read *The Oxford Book of Modern English Verse* and 'Warning' is certainly there, chosen by Larkin himself.

So here is a first-rate selection of some of the greatest poetry of the last hundred years. And I say that, secure in the knowledge that I did not choose these poems, the nation did. (Aspiring poets, of whatever standard, please, please read that last bit again, very carefully. Thank you.)

But having said all that, I am going to break these rules and insert a special poem that nobody voted for. The BBC commissioned a modern version of the poem 'If— ' to be read on television when the results of the poll were announced. It is called 'What If' and was written by Benjamin Zephaniah. Here it is, together with the original Rudyard Kipling poem that inspired its creation.

BENJAMIN ZEPHANIAH 1958–

WHAT IF

If you can keep your money when governments about you
Are losing theirs and blaming it on you.
If you can trust your neighbour when they trust not you
And they be very nosy too;
If you can await the warm delights of summer
Then summer comes and goes with sun not seen,
And pay so much for drinking water
Knowing that the water is unclean.

If you seek peace in times of war creation,
And you can see that oil merchants are to blame,
If you can meet a pimp or politician,
And treat those two impostors just the same;
If you cannot bear dis-united nations
And you think this new world order is a trick,
If you've ever tried to build good race relations,
And watch bad policing mess your work up quick.

If you can make one heap of all your savings
And risk buying a small house and a plot,
Then sit back and watch the economy inflating
Then have to deal with the negative equity you've got.
If you can force your mind and body to continue
When all the social services have gone,
If you struggle on when there is nothing in you,
Except the knowledge that justice cannot be wrong.

If you can speak the truth to common people
Or walk with Kings and Queens and live no lie,
If you can see how power can be evil
And know that every censor is a spy;
If you can fill an unforgiving lifetime
With years of working hard to make ends meet,
You may not be wealthy but I am sure you will find
That you can hold your head high as you walk the streets.

RUDYARD KIPLING 1865–1936

IF—

If you can keep your head when all about you
    Are losing theirs and blaming it on you,
If you can trust yourself when all men doubt you,
    But make allowance for their doubting too;
If you can wait and not be tired by waiting,
    Or being lied about, don't deal in lies,
Or being hated, don't give way to hating,
    And yet don't look too good, nor talk too wise:

If you can dream – and not make dreams your master;
    If you can think – and not make thoughts your aim;
If you can meet with Triumph and Disaster
    And treat those two impostors just the same;
If you can bear to hear the truth you've spoken
    Twisted by knaves to make a trap for fools,
Or watch the things you gave your life to, broken,
    And stoop and build 'em up with worn-out tools:

If you can make one heap of all your winnings
    And risk it on one turn of pitch-and-toss,
And lose, and start again at your beginnings
    And never breathe a word about your loss;
If you can force your heart and nerve and sinew
    To serve your turn long after they are gone,
And so hold on when there is nothing in you
    Except the Will which says to them: 'Hold on!'

If you can talk with crowds and keep your virtue,
    Or walk with Kings – nor lose the common touch
If neither foes nor loving friends can hurt you,
    If all men count with you, but none too much;
If you can fill the unforgiving minute
    With sixty seconds' worth of distance run,
Yours is the Earth and everything that's in it,
    And – which is more – you'll be a Man, my son!

*'His look was a lion's,
Full of rage, defiance'*

from 'My Old Cat'

DYLAN THOMAS 1914–53

_____

DO NOT GO GENTLE INTO THAT GOOD NIGHT

Do not go gentle into that good night,
Old age should burn and rave at close of day;
Rage, rage against the dying of the light.

Though wise men at their end know dark is right,
Because their words had forked no lightning they
Do not go gentle into that good night.

Good men, the last wave by, crying how bright
Their frail deeds might have danced in a green bay,
Rage, rage against the dying of the light.

Wild men who caught and sang the sun in flight,
And learn, too late, they grieved it on its way,
Do not go gentle into that good night.

Grave men, near death, who see with blinding sight
Blind eyes could blaze like meteors and be gay,
Rage, rage against the dying of the light.

And you, my father, there on the sad height,
Curse, bless, me now with your fierce tears, I pray.
Do not go gentle into that good night.
Rage, rage against the dying of the light.

JENNY JOSEPH 1932–

WARNING

When I am an old woman I shall wear purple
With a red hat which doesn't go, and doesn't suit me.
And I shall spend my pension on brandy and summer gloves
And satin sandals, and say we've no money for butter.
I shall sit down on the pavement when I'm tired
And gobble up samples in shops and press alarm bells
And run my stick along the public railings
And make up for the sobriety of my youth.
I shall go out in my slippers in the rain
And pick the flowers in other people's gardens
And learn to spit.

You can wear terrible shirts and grow more fat
And eat three pounds of sausages at a go
Or only bread and pickle for a week
And hoard pens and pencils and beermats and things in boxes.

But now we must have clothes that keep us dry
And pay our rent and not swear in the street
And set a good example for the children.
We must have friends to dinner and read the papers.

But maybe I ought to practise a little now?
So people who know me are not too shocked and surprised
When suddenly I am old, and start to wear purple.

EDMUND BLUNDEN 1896–1974

THE MIDNIGHT SKATERS

The hop-poles stand in cones,
    The icy pond lurks under,
The pole-tops steeple to the thrones
    Of stars, sound gulfs of wonder;
But not the tallest there, 'tis said,
Could fathom to this pond's black bed.

Then is not death at watch
    Within those secret waters?
What wants he but to catch
    Earth's heedless sons and daughters?
With but a crystal parapet
Between, he has his engines set.

Then on, blood shouts, on, on,
    Twirl, wheel and whip above him,
Dance on this ball-floor thin and wan,
    Use him as though you love him;
Court him, elude him, reel and pass,
And let him hate you through the glass.

SYLVIA PLATH 1932–63

LADY LAZARUS

I have done it again.
One year in every ten
I manage it——

A sort of walking miracle, my skin
Bright as a Nazi lampshade,
My right foot

A paperweight,
My face a featureless, fine
Jew linen.

Peel off the napkin
O my enemy.
Do I terrify?——

The nose, the eye pits, the full set of teeth?
The sour breath
Will vanish in a day.

Soon, soon the flesh
The grave cave ate will be
At home on me

And I a smiling woman.
I am only thirty.
And like the cat I have nine times to die.

This is Number Three.
What a trash
To annihilate each decade.

What a million filaments.
The peanut-crunching crowd
Shoves in to see

Them unwrap me hand and foot——
The big strip tease.
Gentlemen, ladies

These are my hands
My knees.
I may be skin and bone,

Nevertheless, I am the same, identical woman.
The first time it happened I was ten.
It was an accident.

The second time I meant
To last it out and not come back at all.
I rocked shut

As a seashell.
They had to call and call
And pick the worms off me like sticky pearls.

Dying
Is an art, like everything else.
I do it exceptionally well.

I do it so it feels like hell.
I do it so it feels real.
I guess you could say I've a call.

It's easy enough to do it in a cell.
It's easy enough to do it and stay put.
It's the theatrical

Comeback in broad day
To the same place, the same face, the same brute
Amused shout:

'A miracle!'
That knocks me out.
There is a charge

For the eyeing of my scars, there is a charge
For the hearing of my heart—
It really goes.

And there is a charge, a very large charge
For a word or a touch
Or a bit of blood

Or a piece of my hair or my clothes.
So, so, Herr Doktor.
So, Herr Enemy.

I am your opus,
I am your valuable,
The pure gold baby

That melts to a shriek.
I turn and burn.
Do not think I underestimate your great concern.

Ash, ash—
You poke and stir.
Flesh, bone, there is nothing there——

A cake of soap,
A wedding ring,
A gold filling.

Herr God, Herr Lucifer
Beware
Beware.

Out of the ash
I rise with my red hair
And I eat men like air.

23–29 October 1962

W.B. YEATS 1865–1939

AN IRISH AIRMAN FORESEES HIS DEATH

I know that I shall meet my fate
Somewhere among the clouds above;
Those that I fight I do not hate,
Those that I guard I do not love;
My country is Kiltartan Cross,
My countrymen Kiltartan's poor,
No likely end could bring them loss
Or leave them happier than before.
Nor law, nor duty bade me fight,
Nor public men, nor cheering crowds,
A lonely impulse of delight
Drove to this tumult in the clouds;
I balanced all, brought all to mind,
The years to come seemed waste of breath,
A waste of breath the years behind
In balance with this life, this death.

MAYA ANGELOU 1928–

PHENOMENAL WOMAN

Pretty women wonder where my secret lies.
I'm not cute or built to suit a fashion model's size
But when I start to tell them,
They think I'm telling lies.
I say,
It's in the reach of my arms,
The span of my hips,
The stride of my step,
The curl of my lips.
I'm a woman
Phenomenally.
Phenomenal woman,
That's me.

I walk into a room
Just as cool as you please,
And to a man,
The fellows stand or
Fall down on their knees.
Then they swarm around me,
A hive of honey bees.
I say,
It's the fire in my eyes,
And the flash of my teeth,
The swing in my waist,
And the joy in my feet.
I'm a woman
Phenomenally.
Phenomenal woman,
That's me.

Men themselves have wondered
What they see in me.
They try so much
But they can't touch
My inner mystery.
When I try to show them
They say they still can't see.
I say,
It's in the arch of my back,
The sun of my smile,
The ride of my breasts,
The grace of my style.
I'm a woman
Phenomenally.
Phenomenal woman,
That's me.

Now you understand
Just why my head's not bowed.
I don't shout or jump about
Or have to talk real loud.
When you see me passing
It ought to make you proud.
I say,
It's in the click of my heels,
The bend of my hair,
the palm of my hand,
The need for my care.
'Cause I'm a woman
Phenomenally.
Phenomenal woman,
That's me.

WILFRED OWEN 1893–1918

DULCE ET DECORUM EST

Bent double, like old beggars under sacks,
Knock-kneed, coughing like hags, we cursed through sludge,
Till on the haunting flares we turned our backs
And towards our distant rest began to trudge.
Men marched asleep. Many had lost their boots
But limped on, blood-shod. All went lame; all blind;
Drunk with fatigue; deaf even to the hoots
Of gas shells dropping softly behind.

Gas! GAS! Quick, boys! – An ecstasy of fumbling,
Fitting the clumsy helmets just in time;
But someone still was yelling out and stumbling,
And flound'ring like a man in fire or lime . . .
Dim, through the misty panes and thick green light,
As under a green sea, I saw him drowning.

In all my dreams, before my helpless sight,
He plunges at me, guttering, choking, drowning.

If in some smothering dreams you too could pace
Behind the wagon that we flung him in,
And watch the white eyes writhing in his face,
His hanging face, like a devil's sick of sin;
If you could hear, at every jolt, the blood
Come gargling from the froth-corrupted lungs,
Obscene as cancer, bitter as the cud
Of vile, incurable sores on innocent tongues, –
My friend, you would not tell with such high zest
To children ardent for some desperate glory,
The old Lie: Dulce et decorum est
Pro patria mori.

SYLVIA PLATH 1932–63

DADDY

You do not do, you do not do
Any more, black shoe
In which I have lived like a foot
For thirty years, poor and white,
Barely daring to breathe or Achoo.

Daddy, I have had to kill you.
You died before I had time—
Marble-heavy, a bag full of God,
Ghastly statue with one grey toe
Big as a Frisco seal

And a head in the freakish Atlantic
Where it pours bean green over blue
In the waters off beautiful Nauset.
I used to pray to recover you.
Ach, du.

In the German tongue, in the Polish town
Scraped flat by the roller
Of wars, wars, wars.
But the name of the town is common.
My Polack friend

Says there are a dozen or two.
So I never could tell where you
Put your foot, your root,
I never could talk to you.
The tongue stuck in my jaw.

It stuck in a barb wire snare.
Ich, ich, ich, ich,
I could hardly speak.
I thought every German was you.
And the language obscene

An engine, an engine
Chuffing me off like a Jew.
A Jew to Dachau, Auschwitz, Belsen.
I began to talk like a Jew.
I think I may well be a Jew.

The snows of the Tyrol, the clear beer of Vienna
Are not very pure or true.
With my gypsy ancestress and my weird luck
And my Taroc pack and my Taroc pack
I may be a bit of a Jew.

I have always been scared of *you*,
With your Luftwaffe, your gobbledygoo.
And your neat moustache
And your Aryan eye, bright blue.
Panzer-man, panzer-man, O You—

Not God but a swastika
So black no sky could squeak through.
Every woman adores a Fascist,
The boot in the face, the brute
Brute heart of a brute like you.

You stand at the blackboard, daddy,
In the picture I have of you,
A cleft in your chin instead of your foot
But no less a devil for that, no not
Any less the black man who

Bit my pretty red heart in two.
I was ten when they buried you.
At twenty I tried to die
And get back, back, back to you.
I thought even the bones would do.

But they pulled me out of the sack,
And they stuck me together with glue.
And then I knew what to do.
I made a model of you,
A man in black with a Meinkampf look.

And a love of the rack and the screw.
And I said I do, I do.
So daddy, I'm finally through.
The black telephone's off at the root,
The voices just can't worm through.

If I've killed one man, I've killed two—
The vampire who said he was you
And drank my blood for a year,
Seven years, if you want to know.
Daddy, you can lie back now.

There's a stake in your fat black heart
And the villagers never liked you.
They are dancing and stamping on you.
They always *knew* it was you.
Daddy, daddy, you bastard, I'm through.

JOHN HEGLEY 1953–

AUTUMN VERSES

Autumn is strange stuff
anagram of Aunt mu
but not of nostalgia.

Scarves come out, clocks go back
faulty or otherwise,
pumpkins enjoy brief popularity.

Kids collecting cash
for slouched-on-the-ground
ash-bound bad dressers.

Ore tummy, heart of mould
old leaves leaving
enter the cold.

Last October
I got very depressed
when our dog got knoctober.

HAL SUMMERS 1911–

MY OLD CAT

My old cat is dead,
Who would butt me with his head.
He had the sleekest fur.
He had the blackest purr.
Always gentle with us
Was this black puss,
But when I found him today
Stiff and cold where he lay
His look was a lion's,
Full of rage, defiance:
Oh, he would not pretend
That what came was a friend
But met it in pure hate.
Well died, my old cat.

MAYA ANGELOU 1928–

STILL I RISE

You may write me down in history
With your bitter, twisted lies,
You may trod me in the very dirt
But still, like dust, I'll rise.

Does my sassiness upset you?
Why are you beset with gloom?
'Cause I walk like I've got oil wells
Pumping in my living room.

Just like moons and like suns,
With the certainty of tides,
Just like hopes springing high,
Still I'll rise.

Did you want to see me broken?
Bowed head and lowered eyes?
Shoulders falling down like teardrops,
Weakened by my soulful cries.

Does my haughtiness offend you?
Don't you take it awful hard
'Cause I laugh like I've got gold mines
Diggin' in my own back yard.

You may shoot me with your words,
You may cut me with your eyes,
You may kill me with your hatefulness,
But still, like air, I'll rise.

Does my sexiness upset you?
Does it come as a surprise
That I dance like I've got diamonds
At the meeting of my thighs?

Out of the huts of history's shame
I rise
Up from a past that's rooted in pain
I rise
I'm a black ocean, leaping and wide,
Welling and swelling I bear in the tide.

Leaving behind nights of terror and fear
I rise
Into a daybreak that's wondrously clear
I rise
Bringing the gifts that my ancestors gave,
I am the dream and the hope of the slave.
I rise
I rise
I rise.

'What will survive of us is love'

from 'An Arundel Tomb'

PHILIP LARKIN 1922–85

AN ARUNDEL TOMB

Side by side, their faces blurred,
The earl and countess lie in stone,
Their proper habits vaguely shown
As jointed armour, stiffened pleat,
And that faint hint of the absurd –
The little dogs under their feet.

Such plainness of the pre-baroque
Hardly involves the eye, until
It meets his left-hand gauntlet, still
Clasped empty in the other; and
One sees, with a sharp tender shock,
His hand withdrawn, holding her hand.

They would not think to lie so long.
Such faithfulness in effigy
Was just a detail friends would see:
A sculptor's sweet commissioned grace
Thrown off in helping to prolong
The Latin names around the base.

They would not guess how early in
Their supine stationary voyage
The air would change to soundless damage,
Turn the old tenantry away;
How soon succeeding eyes begin
To look, not read. Rigidly they

Persisted, linked, through lengths and breadths
Of time. Snow fell, undated. Light
Each summer thronged the glass. A bright
Litter of birdcalls strewed the same
Bone-riddled ground. And up the paths
The endless altered people came,

Washing at their identity.
Now, helpless in the hollow of
An unarmorial age, a trough
Of smoke in slow suspended skeins
Above their scrap of history,
Only an attitude remains:

Time has transfigured them into
Untruth. The stone fidelity
They hardly meant has come to be
Their final blazon, and to prove
Our almost-instinct almost true:
What will survive of us is love.

E.E. CUMMINGS 1894–1962

SOMEWHERE I HAVE NEVER TRAVELLED

somewhere i have never travelled,gladly beyond
any experience,your eyes have their silence:
in your most frail gesture are things which enclose me,
or which i cannot touch because they are too near

your slightest look easily will unclose me
though i have closed myself as fingers,
you open always petal by petal myself as Spring opens
(touching skilfully,mysteriously)her first rose

or if your wish be to close me,i and
my life will shut very beautifully,suddenly,
as when the heart of this flower imagines
the snow carefully everywhere descending;

nothing which we are to perceive in this world equals
the power of your intense fragility:whose texture
compels me with the colour of its countries,
rendering death and forever with each breathing

(i do not know what it is about you that closes
and opens;only something in me understands
the voice of your eyes is deeper than all roses)
nobody,not even the rain,has such small hands

SIR JOHN BETJEMAN 1906–84

A SUBALTERN'S LOVE-SONG

Miss J. Hunter Dunn, Miss J. Hunter Dunn,
Furnish'd and burnish'd by Aldershot sun,
What strenuous singles we played after tea,
We in the tournament – you against me!

Love-thirty, love-forty, oh! weakness of joy,
The speed of a swallow, the grace of a boy,
With carefullest carelessness, gaily you won,
I am weak from your loveliness, Joan Hunter Dunn.

Miss Joan Hunter Dunn, Miss Joan Hunter Dunn,
How mad I am, sad I am, glad that you won.
The warm-handled racket is back in its press,
But my shock-headed victor, she loves me no less.

Her father's euonymus shines as we walk,
And swing past the summer-house, buried in talk,
And cool the verandah that welcomes us in
To the six-o'clock news and a lime-juice and gin.

The scent of the conifers, sound of the bath,
The view from my bedroom of moss-dappled path,
As I struggle with double-end evening tie,
For we dance at the Golf Club, my victor and I.

On the floor of her bedroom lie blazer and shorts
And the cream-coloured walls are be-trophied with sports,
And westering, questioning settles the sun
On your low-leaded window, Miss Joan Hunter Dunn.

The Hillman is waiting, the light's in the hall,
The pictures of Egypt are bright on the wall,
My sweet, I am standing beside the oak stair
And there on the landing's the light on your hair.

By roads 'not adopted', by woodlanded ways,
She drove to the club in the late summer haze,
Into nine-o'clock Camberley, heavy with bells
And mushroomy, pine-woody, evergreen smells.

Miss Joan Hunter Dunn, Miss Joan Hunter Dunn,
I can hear from the car-park the dance has begun.
Oh! full Surrey twilight! importunate band!
Oh! strongly adorable tennis-girl's hand!

Around us are Rovers and Austins afar,
Above us, the intimate roof of the car,
And here on my right is the girl of my choice,
With the tilt of her nose and the chime of her voice,

And the scent of her wrap, and the words never said,
And the ominous, ominous dancing ahead.
We sat in the car park till twenty to one
And now I'm engaged to Miss Joan Hunter Dunn.

W.H. AUDEN 1907–73

CARRY HER OVER THE WATER

Carry her over the water,
  And set her down under the tree,
Where the culvers white all day and all night,
  And the winds from every quarter
Sing agreeably, agreeably, agreeably of love.

Put a gold ring on her finger,
  And press her close to your heart,
While the fish in the lake their snapshots take,
  And the frog, that sanguine singer,
Sing agreeably, agreeably, agreeably of love.

The streets shall all flock to your marriage,
  The houses turn round to look,
The tables and chairs say suitable prayers,
  And the horses drawing your carriage
Sing agreeably, agreeably, agreeably of love.

JON STALLWORTHY 1935–

THE ALMOND TREE

I

All the way to the hospital
the lights were green as peppermints.
Trees of black iron broke into leaf
ahead of me, as if
I were the lucky prince
in an enhanted wood
summoning summer with my whistle,
banishing winter with a nod.

Swung by the road from bend to bend,
I was aware that blood was running
down through the delta of my wrist
and under arches
of bright bone. Centuries,
continents it had crossed;
from an undiscovered beginning
spiralling to an unmapped end.

II

Crossing (at sixty) Magdalen Bridge
Let it be a son, a son, said
the man in the driving mirror,
Let it be a son. The tower
held up its hand: the college
bells shook their blessing on his head.

III

I parked in an almond's
shadow blossom, for the tree
was waving, waving me
upstairs with a child's hands.

IV

Up
the spinal stair
and at the top
along
a bone-white corridor
the blood tide swung
me swung me to a room
whose walls shuddered
with the shuddering womb.
Under the sheet
wave after wave, wave
after wave beat
on the bone coast, bringing
ashore – whom?
New-
minted, my bright farthing!
Coined by our love, stamped with
our images, how you
enrich us! Both
you make one. Welcome
to your white sheet,
my best poem!

V

At seven-thirty
the visitors' bell
scissored the calm
of the corridors.
The doctor walked with me
to the slicing doors.
His hand upon my arm,
his voice – *I have to tell*
you – set another bell
beating in my head:
your son is a mongol
the doctor said.

VI

How easily the word went in –
clean as a bullet
leaving no mark on the skin,
stopping the heart within it.

This was my first death.
The '*I*' ascending on a slow
last thermal breath
studied the man below

as a pilot treading air might
the buckled shell of his plane –
boot, glove, helmet
feeling no pain

from the snapped wires' radiant ends.
Looking down from a thousand feet
I held four walls in the lens
of an eye: wall, window, the street

a torrent of windscreens, my own
car under its almond tree,
and the almond waving me down.
I wrestled against gravity.

but light was melting and the gulf
cracked open. Unfamiliar
the body of my late self
I carried to the car.

VII

The hospital – its heavy freight
lashed down ship-shape ward over ward –
steamed into night with some on board
soon to be lost if the desperate

charts were known. Others would come
altered to land or find the land
altered. At their voyage's end
some would be added to, some

diminished. In a numbered cot
my son sailed from me; never to come
ashore into my kingdom
speaking my language. Better not

look that way. The almond tree
was beautiful in labour. Blood-
dark, quickening, bud after bud
split, flower after flower shook free.

On the darkening wind a pale
face floated. Out of reach. Only when
the buds, all the buds, were broken
would the tree be in full sail.

In labour the tree was becoming
itself. I, too, rooted in earth
and ringed by darkness, from the death
of myself saw myself blossoming,

wrenched from the caul of my thirty
years' growing, fathered by my son,
unkindly in a kind season
by love shattered and set free.

LOUIS MACNEICE 1907–63

MEETING POINT

Time was away and somewhere else,
There were two glasses and two chairs
And two people with the one pulse
(Somebody stopped the moving stairs):
Time was away and somewhere else.

And they were neither up nor down;
The stream's music did not stop
Flowing through heather, limpid brown,
Although they sat in a coffee shop
And they were neither up nor down.

The bell was silent in the air
Holding its inverted poise –
Between the clang and clang a flower,
A brazen calyx of no noise:
The bell was silent in the air.

The camels crossed the miles of sand
That stretched around the cups and plates;
The desert was their own, they planned
To portion out the stars and dates:
The camels crossed the miles of sand.

Time was away and somewhere else.
The waiter did not come, the clock
Forgot them and the radio waltz
Came out like water from a rock:
Time was away and somewhere else.

Her fingers flicked away the ash
That bloomed again in tropic trees:
Not caring if the markets crash
When they had forests such as these,
Her fingers flicked away the ash.

God or whatever means the Good
Be praised that time can stop like this,
That what the heart has understood
Can verify in the body's peace
God or whatever means the Good.

Time was away and she was here
And life no longer what it was,
The bell was silent in the air
And all the room one glow because
Time was away and she was here.

April, 1939

ADRIAN HENRI 1932–

WITHOUT YOU

Without you every morning would be like going back to work
    after a holiday,
Without you I couldn't stand the smell of the East Lancs Road,
Without you ghost ferries would cross the Mersey manned by
    skeleton crews,
Without you I'd probably feel happy and have more money
    and time and nothing to do with it,
Without you I'd have to leave my stillborn poems on other
    people's doorsteps, wrapped in brown paper,
Without you there'd never be sauce to put on sausage butties,
Without you plastic flowers in shop windows would just be
    plastic flowers in shop windows
Without you I'd spend my summers picking morosely over
    the remains of train crashes,
Without you white birds would wrench themselves free from
    my paintings and fly off dripping blood into the night,
Without you green apples wouldn't taste greener,
Without you Mothers wouldn't let their children play out after
    tea,
Without you every musician in the world would forget how to
    play the blues,
Without you Public Houses would be public again,
Without you the Sunday Times colour supplement would
    come out in black-and-white,
Without you indifferent colonels would shrug their shoulders
    and press the button,
Without you they'd stop changing the flowers in Piccadilly
    Gardens,
Without you Clark Kent would forget how to become
    Superman,
Without you Sunshine Breakfast would only consist of
    Cornflakes,
Without you there'd be no colour in Magic colouring books,

Without you Mahler's 8th would only be performed by street
    musicians in derelict houses,
Without you they'd forget to put the salt in every packet of
    crisps,
Without you it would be an offence punishable by a fine of up
    to £200 or two months' imprisonment to be found in
    possession of curry powder,
Without you riot police are massing in quiet sidestreets,
Without you all streets would be one-way the other way,
Without you there'd be no one not to kiss goodnight when we
    quarrel,
Without you the first martian to land would turn round and go
    away again,
Without you they'd forget to change the weather,
Without you blind men would sell unlucky heather,
Without you there would be
no landscapes/no stations/no houses,
no chipshops/no quiet villages/no seagulls
on beaches/no hopscotch on pavements/no night/no morning/
    there'd be no city no country
Without you.

ANON

FOOTPRINTS

One night a man had a dream,
He dreamed he was walking along the beach with the LORD.
Across the sky flashed scenes from his life.
For each scene, he noticed two sets of footprints in the sand,
One belonging to him and the other to the LORD.
When the last scene of his life flashed before him
He looked back at the footprints in the sand.
He noticed that many times along the path of his life
There was only one set of footprints.
He also noticed that it happened at the very lowest and saddest times
   in his life.
This really bothered him and he questioned the LORD about it:
'LORD, you said that once I decided to follow you, you'd walk with
   me all the way.
But I have noticed that during the most troublesome times in my life,
There was only one set of footprints.
I don't understand why when I needed you most you would leave me.'
The LORD replied:
'My son, my precious child, I love you and I would never leave you.
   During your times of trial and suffering, when you see only one
   set of footprints, it was then that I carried you.'

DYLAN THOMAS 1914–53

from UNDER MILK WOOD

ROSIE PROBERT *(Softly)*
What seas did you see,
Tom Cat, Tom Cat,
In your sailoring days
Long long ago?
What sea beasts were
In the wavery green
When you were my master?

CAPTAIN CAT
I'll tell you the truth.
Seas barking like seals,
Blue seas and green,
Seas covered with eels
And mermen and whales.

ROSIE PROBERT
What seas did you sail
Old whaler when
On the blubbery waves
Between Frisco and Wales
You were my bosun?

CAPTAIN CAT
As true as I'm here
Dear you Tom Cat's tart
You landlubber Rosie
You cosy love
My easy as easy
My true sweetheart,
Seas green as a bean
Seas gliding with swans
In the seal-barking moon.

ROSIE PROBERT
    What seas were rocking
    My little deck hand
    My favourite husband
    In your seaboots and hunger
    My duck my whaler
    My honey my daddy
    My pretty sugar sailor.
    With my name on your belly
    When you were a boy
    Long long ago?

CAPTAIN CAT
    I'll tell you no lies.
    The only sea I saw
    Was the seesaw sea
    With you riding on it.
    Lie down, lie easy.
    Let me shipwreck in your thighs.

ROSIE PROBERT
    Knock twice, Jack,
    At the door of my grave
    And ask for Rosie.

CAPTAIN CAT
    Rosie Probert.

ROSIE PROBERT
    Remember her.
    She is forgetting.
    The earth which filled her mouth
    Is vanishing from her.
    Remember me.
    I have forgotten you.
    I am going into the darkness of the darkness for ever.
    I have forgotten that I was ever born.

STEVIE SMITH 1902–71

THE SINGING CAT

It was a little captive cat
　　Upon a crowded train
His mistress takes him from his box
　　To ease his fretful pain.

She holds him tight upon her knee
　　The graceful animal
And all the people look at him
　　He is so beautiful.

But oh he pricks and oh he prods
　　And turns upon her knee
Then lifteth up his innocent voice
　　In plaintive melody.

He lifteth up his innocent voice
　　He lifteth up, he singeth
And to each human countenance
　　A smile of grace he bringeth.

He lifteth up his innocent paw
　　Upon her breast he clingeth
And everybody cries, Behold
　　The cat, the cat that singeth.

He lifteth up his innocent voice
　　He lifteth up, he singeth
And all the people warm themselves
　　In the love his beauty bringeth.

EDWIN MORGAN 1920–

STRAWBERRIES

There were never strawberries
like the ones we had
that sultry afternoon
sitting on the step
of the open french window
facing each other
your knees held in mine
the blue plates in our laps
the strawberries glistening
in the hot sunlight
we dipped them in sugar
looking at each other
not hurrying the feast
for one to come
the empty plates
laid on the stone together
with the two forks crossed
and I bent towards you
sweet in that air
in my arms
abandoned like a child
from your eager mouth
the taste of strawberries
in my memory
lean back again
let me love you

let the sun beat
on our forgetfulness
one hour of all
the heat intense
and summer lightning
on the Kilpatrick hills

let the storm wash the plates

ROGER McGOUGH 1937–

VINEGAR

sometimes
i feel like a priest
in a fish & chip queue
quietly thinking
as the vinegar runs through
how nice it would be
to buy supper for two

SIR JOHN BETJEMAN 1906–84

MYFANWY

Kind o'er the *kinderbank* leans my Myfanwy,
  White o'er the play-pen the sheen of her dress,
Fresh from the bathroom and soft in the nursery
  Soap-scented fingers I long to caress.

Were you a prefect and head of your dormit'ry?
  Were you a hockey girl, tennis or gym?
Who was your favourite? Who had a crush on you?
  Which were the baths where they taught you to swim?

Smooth down the Avenue glitters the bicycle,
  Black-stockinged legs under navy-blue serge,
Home and Colonial, Star, International,
  Balancing bicycle leant on the verge.

Trace me your wheel-tracks, you fortunate bicycle,
  Out of the shopping and into the dark,
Back down the Avenue, back to the pottingshed,
  Back to the house on the fringe of the park.

Golden the light on the locks of Myfanwy,
  Golden the light on the book on her knee,
Finger-marked pages of Rackham's Hans Andersen,
  Time for the children to come down to tea.

Oh! Fuller's angel-cake, Robertson's marmalade,
  Liberty lampshade, come, shine on us all,
My! what a spread for the friends of Myfanwy
  Some in the alcove and some in the hall.

Then what sardines in the half-lighted passages!
  Locking of fingers in long hide-and-seek.
You will protect me, my silken Myfanwy,
  Ringleader, tom-boy, and chum to the weak.

W.B. YEATS 1865–1939

HE WISHES FOR THE CLOTHS OF HEAVEN

Had I the heavens' embroidered cloths,
Enwrought with golden and silver light,
The blue and the dim and the dark cloths
Of night and light and the half-light,
I would spread the cloths under your feet:
But I, being poor, have only my dreams;
I have spread my dreams under your feet;
Tread softly because you tread on my dreams.

' . . . we have no hope of better
Happiness than this, . . . '

from 'Modern Love'

HUGO WILLIAMS 1942–

TIDES

The evening advances, then withdraws again
Leaving our cups and books like islands on the floor.
We are drifting you and I,
As far from one another as the young heroes
Of these two novels we have just laid down.
For that is happiness: to wander alone
Surrounded by the same moon, whose tides remind us of
ourselves,
Our distances, and what we leave behind.
The lamp left on, the curtains letting in the light.
These things were promises. No doubt we will come back to
them.

WENDY COPE 1945–

LOSS

The day he moved out was terrible –
That evening she went through hell.
His absence wasn't a problem
But the corkscrew had gone as well.

ROGER McGOUGH 1937–

COMECLOSE AND SLEEPNOW

it is afterwards
and you talk on tiptoe
happy to be part
of the darkness
lips becoming limp
a prelude to tiredness.
Comeclose and Sleepnow
for in the morning
when a policeman
disguised as the sun
creeps into the room
and your mother
disguised as birds
calls from the trees
you will put on a dress of guilt
and shoes with broken high ideals
and refusing coffee
run
alltheway
home.

BRIAN PATTEN 1946–

PORTRAIT OF A YOUNG GIRL RAPED
AT A SUBURBAN PARTY

And after this quick bash in the dark
You will rise and go
Thinking of how empty you have grown
And of whether all the evening's care in front of mirrors
And the younger boys disowned
Led simply to this.

Confined to what you are expected to be
By what you are
Out in this frozen garden
You shiver and vomit –
Frightened, drunk among trees,
You wonder at how those acts that called for tenderness
Were far from tender.

Now you have left your titterings about love
And your childishness behind you
Yet still far from being old
You spew up among flowers
And in the warm stale rooms
The party continues.

It seems you saw some use in moving away
From that group of drunken lives
Yet already ten minutes pregnant
In twenty thousand you might remember
This party
This dull Saturday evening
When planets rolled out of your eyes
And splashed down in suburban grasses.

DOUGLAS DUNN 1942–

MODERN LOVE

It is summer, and we are in a house
That is not ours, sitting at a table
Enjoying minutes of a rented silence,
The upstairs people gone. The pigeons lull
To sleep the under-tens and invalids,
The tree shakes out its shadows to the grass,
The roses rove through the wilds of my neglect.
Our lives flap, and we have no hope of better
Happiness than this, not much to show for love
But how we are, or how this evening is,
Unpeopled, silent, and where we are alive
In a domestic love, seemingly alone,
All other lives worn down to trees and sunlight,
Looking forward to a visit from the cat.

ALICE WALKER 1944–

DID THIS HAPPEN TO YOUR MOTHER?
DID YOUR SISTER THROW UP A LOT?

I love a man who is not worth
my love.
Did this happen to your mother?
Did your grandmother wake up
for no good reason
in the middle of the night?

I thought love could be controlled.
It cannot.
Only behavior can be controlled.
By biting your tongue purple
rather than speak.
Mauling your lips.
Obliterating his number
too thoroughly
to be able to phone.

Love has made me sick.

Did your sister throw up a lot?
Did your cousin complain
of a painful knot
in her back?
Did your aunt always
seem to have something else
troubling her mind?

I thought love would adapt itself
to my needs.
But needs grow too fast;
they come up like weeds.
Through cracks in the conversation.
Through silences in the dark.
Through everything you thought was concrete.

70

Such needful love has to be chopped out
or forced to wilt back,
poisoned by disapproval
from its own soil.

This is bad news, for the conservationist.

My hand shakes before this killing.
My stomach sits jumpy in my chest.
My chest is the Grand Canyon
sprawled empty
over the world.

Whoever he is, he is not worth all this.

And I will never
unclench my teeth long enough
to tell him so.

PHILIP LARKIN 1922–85

DECEPTIONS

'Of course I was drugged, and so heavily I
did not regain my consciousness till the next
morning. I was horrified to discover that I
had been ruined, and for some days I was
inconsolable, and cried like a child to be
killed or sent back to my aunt.'

Mayhew, *London Labour and the London Poor.*

Even so distant, I can taste the grief,
Bitter and sharp with stalks, he made you gulp.
The sun's occasional print, the brisk brief
Worry of wheels along the street outside
Where bridal London bows the other way,
And light, unanswerable and tall and wide,
Forbids the scar to heal, and drives
Shame out of hiding. All the unhurried day
Your mind lay open like a drawer of knives.

Slums, years, have buried you. I would not dare
Console you if I could. What can be said,
Except that suffering is exact, but where
Desire takes charge, readings will grow erratic?
For you would hardly care
That you were less deceived, out on that bed,
Than he was, stumbling up the breathless stair
To burst into fulfilment's desolate attic.

BRIAN PATTEN 1946–

A BLADE OF GRASS

You ask for a poem.
I offer you a blade of grass.
You say it is not good enough.
You ask for a poem.

I say this blade of grass will do.
It has dressed itself in frost,
It is more immediate
Than any image of my making.

You say it is not a poem,
It is a blade of grass and grass
Is not quite good enough.
I offer you a blade of grass.

You are indignant.
You say it is too easy to offer grass.
It is absurd.
Anyone can offer a blade of grass.

You ask for a poem.
And so I write you a tragedy about
How a blade of grass
Becomes more and more difficult to offer,

And about how as you grow older
A blade of grass
Becomes more difficult to accept.

WENDY COPE 1945–

A CHRISTMAS POEM

At Christmas little children sing and merry bells
  jingle,
The cold winter air makes our hands and faces
  tingle
And happy families go to church and cheerily they
  mingle
And the whole business is unbelievably dreadful, if
  you're single.

'In labour-saving homes, with care
Their wives frizz out peroxide hair'

from 'Slough'

CRAIG RAINE 1944–

A MARTIAN SENDS A POSTCARD HOME

Caxtons are mechanical birds with many wings
and some are treasured for their markings –

they cause the eyes to melt
or the body to shriek without pain.

I have never seen one fly, but
sometimes they perch on the hand.

Mist is when the sky is tired of flight
and rests its soft machine on ground:

then the world is dim and bookish
like engravings under tissue paper.

Rain is when the earth is television.
It has the property of making colours darker.

Model T is a room with the lock inside –
a key is turned to free the world

for movement, so quick there is a film
to watch for anything missed.

But time is tied to the wrist
or kept in a box, ticking with impatience.

In homes, a haunted apparatus sleeps,
that snores when you pick it up.

If the ghost cries, they carry it
to their lips and soothe it to sleep

with sounds. And yet, they wake it up
deliberately, by tickling with a finger.

Only the young are allowed to suffer
openly. Adults go to a punishment room

with water but nothing to eat.
They lock the door and suffer the noises

alone. No one is exempt
and everyone's pain has a different smell.

At night, when all the colours die,
they hide in pairs

and read about themselves –
in colour, with their eyelids shut.

PHILIP LARKIN 1922–85

TOADS

Why should I let the toad *work*
    Squat on my life?
Can't I use my wit as a pitchfork
    And drive the brute off?

Six days of the week it soils
    With its sickening poison –
Just for paying a few bills!
    That's out of proportion.

Lots of folk live on their wits:
    Lecturers, lispers,
Losels, loblolly-men, louts –
    They don't end as paupers;

Lots of folk live up lanes
    With fires in a bucket,
Eat windfalls and tinned sardines –
    They seem to like it.

Their nippers have got bare feet,
    Their unspeakable wives
Are skinny as whippets – and yet
    No one actually *starves*.

Ah, were I courageous enough
    To shout *Stuff your pension!*
But I know, all too well, that's the stuff
    That dreams are made on:

For something sufficiently toad-like
   Squats in me, too;
Its hunkers are heavy as hard luck,
   And cold as snow,

And will never allow me to blarney
   My way to getting
The fame and the girl and the money
   All at one sitting.

I don't say, one bodies the other
   One's spiritual truth;
But I do say it's hard to lose either,
   When you have both.

W.H. AUDEN 1907–73

NIGHT MAIL

I

This is the Night Mail crossing the Border,
Bringing the cheque and the postal order,

Letters for the rich, letters for the poor,
The shop at the corner, the girl next door.

Pulling up Beattock, a steady climb:
The gradient's against her, but she's on time.

Past cotton-grass and moorland boulder,
Shovelling white steam over her shoulder,

Snorting noisily, she passes
Silent miles of wind-bent grasses.

Birds turn their heads as she approaches,
Stare from bushes at her blank-faced coaches.

Sheep-dogs cannot turn her course;
They slumber on with paws across.

In the farm she passes no one wakes,
But a jug in a bedroom gently shakes.

II

Dawn freshens. Her climb is done.
Down towards Glasgow she descends,
Towards the steam tugs yelping down a glade of cranes,
Towards the fields of apparatus, the furnaces
Set on the dark plain like gigantic chessmen.
All Scotland waits for her:
In dark glens, beside pale-green lochs,
Men long for news.

III

Letters of thanks, letters from banks,
Letters of joy from girl and boy,
Receipted bills and invitations
To inspect new stock or to visit relations,
And applications for situations,
And timid lovers' declarations,
And gossip, gossip from all the nations,
News circumstantial, news financial,
Letters with holiday snaps to enlarge in,
Letters with faces scrawled on the margin,
Letters from uncles, cousins and aunts,
Letters to Scotland from the South of France,
Letters of condolence to Highlands and Lowlands,
Written on paper of every hue,
The pink, the violet, the white and the blue,
The chatty, the catty, the boring, the adoring,
The cold and official and the heart's outpouring,
Clever, stupid, short and long,
The typed and the printed and the spelt all wrong.

IV

Thousands are still asleep,
Dreaming of terrifying monsters
Or a friendly tea beside the band in Cranston's or Crawford's:
Asleep in working Glasgow, asleep in well-set Edinburgh,
Asleep in granite Aberdeen,
They continue their dreams,
But shall wake soon and hope for letters,
And none will hear the postman's knock
Without a quickening of the heart.
For who can bear to feel himself forgotten?

PHILIP LARKIN 1922–85

GOING, GOING

I thought it would last my time –
The sense that, beyond the town,
There would always be fields and farms,
Where the village louts could climb
Such trees as were not cut down;
I knew there'd be false alarms

In the papers about old streets
And split-level shopping, but some
Have always been left so far;
And when the old parts retreat
As the bleak high-risers come
We can always escape in the car.

Things are tougher than we are, just
As earth will always respond
However we mess it about;
Chuck filth in the sea, if you must:
The tides will be clean beyond.
– But what do I feel now? Doubt?

Or age, simply? The crowd
Is young in the M1 café;
Their kids are screaming for more –
More houses, more parking allowed,
More caravan sites, more pay:
On the Business Page, a score

Of spectacled grins approve
Some takeover bid that entails
Five per cent profit (and ten
Per cent more in the estuaries): move
Your works to the unspoilt dales
(Grey area grants)! And when

You try to get near the sea
In summer . . .
                    It seems, just now,
To be happening so very fast;
Despite all the land left free
For the first time I feel somehow
That it isn't going to last,

That before I snuff it, the whole
Boiling will be bricked in
Except for the tourist parts –
First slum of Europe: a role
It won't be so hard to win,
With a cast of crooks and tarts.

And that will be England gone,
The shadows, the meadows, the lanes,
The guildhalls, the carved choirs.
There'll be books; it will linger on
In galleries; but all that remains
For us will be concrete and tyres.

Most things are never meant.
This won't be, most likely: but greeds
And garbage are too thick-strewn
To be swept up now, or invent
Excuses that make them all needs.
I just think it will happen, soon.

ROBERT GRAVES 1895–1985

WELSH INCIDENT

'But that was nothing to what things came out
From the sea-caves of Criccieth yonder.'
'What were they? Mermaids? dragons? ghosts?'
'Nothing at all of any things like that.'
'What were they, then?'
                     'All sorts of queer things,
Things never seen or heard or written about,
Very strange, un-Welsh, utterly peculiar
Things. Oh, solid enough they seemed to touch,
Had anyone dared it. Marvellous creation,
All various shapes and sizes, and no sizes,
All new, each perfectly unlike his neighbour,
Though all came moving slowly out together.'
'Describe just one of them.'
                  'I am unable.'
'What were their colours?'
                  'Mostly nameless colours,
Colours you'd like to see; but one was puce
Or perhaps more like crimson, but not purplish.
Some had no colour.'
                'Tell me, had they legs?'
'Not a leg or foot among them that I saw.'
'But did these things come out in any order?
What o'clock was it? What was the day of the week?
Who else was present? How was the weather?'
'I was coming to that. It was half-past three
On Easter Tuesday last. The sun was shining.
The Harlech Silver Band played *Marchog Jesu*
On thirty-seven shimmering instruments,
Collecting for Caernarvon's (Fever) Hospital Fund.
The populations of Pwllheli, Criccieth,
Portmadoc, Borth, Tremadoc, Penrhyndeudraeth,
Were all assembled. Criccieth's mayor addressed them

First in good Welsh and then in fluent English,
Twisting his fingers in his chain of office,
Welcoming the things. They came out on the sand,
Not keeping time to the band, moving seaward
Silently at a snail's pace. But at last
The most odd, indescribable thing of all
Which hardly one man there could see for wonder
Did something recognizably a something.'
'Well, what?'
             'It made a noise.'
                           'A frightening noise?'
'No, no.'
             'A musical noise? A noise of scuffling?'
'No, but a very loud, respectable noise –
Like groaning to oneself on Sunday morning
In Chapel, close before the second psalm.'
'What did the mayor do?'
                         'I was coming to that.'

PHILIP LARKIN 1922–85

THE WHITSUN WEDDINGS

That Whitsun, I was late getting away:
   Not till about
One-twenty on the sunlit Saturday
Did my three-quarters-empty train pull out,
All windows down, all cushions hot, all sense
Of being in a hurry gone. We ran
Behind the backs of houses, crossed a street
Of blinding windscreens, smelt the fish-dock; thence
The river's level drifting breadth began,
Where sky and Lincolnshire and water meet.

All afternoon, through the tall heat that slept
   For miles inland,
A slow and stopping curve southwards we kept.
Wide farms went by, short-shadowed cattle, and
Canals with floatings of industrial froth;
A hothouse flashed uniquely: hedges dipped
And rose: and now and then a smell of grass
Displaced the reek of buttoned carriage-cloth
Until the next town, new and nondescript,
Approached with acres of dismantled cars.

At first, I didn't notice what a noise
   The weddings made
Each station that we stopped at: sun destroys
The interest of what's happening in the shade,
And down the long cool platforms whoops and skirls
I took for porters larking with the mails,
And went on reading. Once we started, though,
We passed them, grinning and pomaded, girls
In parodies of fashion, heels and veils,
All posed irresolutely, watching us go,

As if out on the end of an event
   Waving goodbye
To something that survived it. Struck, I leant
More promptly out next time, more curiously,
And saw it all again in different terms:
The fathers with broad belts under their suits
And seamy foreheads; mothers loud and fat;
An uncle shouting smut; and then the perms,
The nylon gloves and jewellery-substitutes,
The lemons, mauves, and olive-ochres that

Marked off the girls unreally from the rest.
   Yes, from cafés
And banquet-halls up yards, and bunting-dressed
Coach-party annexes, the wedding-days
Were coming to an end. All down the line
Fresh couples climbed aboard: the rest stood round;
The last confetti and advice were thrown,
And, as we moved, each face seemed to define
Just what it saw departing: children frowned
At something dull; fathers had never known

Success so huge and wholly farcical;
   The women shared
The secret like a happy funeral;
While girls, gripping their handbags tighter, stared
At a religious wounding. Free at last,
And loaded with the sum of all they saw,
We hurried towards London, shuffling gouts of steam.
Now fields were building-plots, and poplars cast
Long shadows over major roads, and for
Some fifty minutes, that in time would seem

Just long enough to settle hats and say
   I nearly died,
A dozen marriages got under way.
They watched the landscape, sitting side by side
– An Odeon went past, a cooling tower,
And someone running up to bowl – and none
Thought of the others they would never meet
Or how their lives would all contain this hour.
I thought of London spread out in the sun,
Its postal districts packed like squares of wheat:

There we were aimed. And as we raced across
   Bright knots of rail
Past standing Pullmans, walls of blackened moss
Came close, and it was nearly done, this frail
Travelling coincidence; and what it held
Stood ready to be loosed with all the power
That being changed can give. We slowed again,
And as the tightened brakes took hold, there swelled
A sense of falling, like an arrow-shower
Sent out of sight, somewhere becoming rain.

SIR JOHN BETJEMAN 1906–84

SLOUGH

Come, friendly bombs, and fall on Slough
It isn't fit for humans now,
There isn't grass to graze a cow
    Swarm over, Death!

Come, bombs, and blow to smithereens
Those air-conditioned, bright canteens,
Tinned fruit, tinned meat, tinned milk, tinned beans
    Tinned minds, tinned breath.

Mess up the mess they call a town –
A house for ninety-seven down
And once a week a half-a-crown
    For twenty years,

And get that man with double chin
Who'll always cheat and always win,
Who washes his repulsive skin
    In women's tears,

And smash his desk of polished oak
And smash his hands so used to stroke
And stop his boring dirty joke
    And make him yell.

But spare the bald young clerks who add
The profits of the stinking cad;
It's not their fault that they are made,
    They've tasted Hell.

It's not their fault they do not know
The birdsong from the radio,
It's not their fault they often go
    To Maidenhead

And talk of sports and makes of cars
In various bogus Tudor bars
And daren't look up and see the stars
　　But belch instead.

In labour-saving homes, with care
Their wives frizz out peroxide hair
And dry it in synthetic air
　　And paint their nails.

Come, friendly bombs, and fall on Slough
To get it ready for the plough.
The cabbages are coming now;
　　The earth exhales.

'For human beings only do
What their religion tells them to'

from 'Diary of a Church Mouse'

SIR JOHN BETJEMAN 1906–84

IN WESTMINSTER ABBEY

Let me take this other glove off
　As the *vox humana* swells,
And the beauteous fields of Eden
　Bask beneath the Abbey bells.
Here, where England's statesmen lie,
Listen to a Lady's cry.

Gracious Lord, oh bomb the Germans.
　Spare their women for Thy Sake.
And if that is not too easy
　We will pardon Thy Mistake.
But, gracious Lord, whate'er shall be,
Don't let anyone bomb me.

Keep our Empire undismembered
　Guide our Forces by Thy Hand,
Gallant blacks from far Jamaica,
　Honduras and Togoland;
Protect them Lord in all their fights,
And, even more, protect the whites.

Think of what our Nation stands for,
　Books from Boots' and country lanes,
Free speech, free passes, class distinction,
　Democracy and proper drains.
Lord, put beneath Thy special care
One-eighty-nine Cadogan Square.

Although dear Lord I am a sinner,
　I have done no major crime;
Now I'll come to Evening Service
　Whensoever I have the time.
So, Lord, reserve for me a crown,
　And do not let my shares go down.

I will labour for Thy Kingdom,
    Help our lads to win the war,
Send white feathers to the cowards
    Join the Women's Army Corps,
Then wash the Steps around Thy Throne
In the Eternal Safety Zone.

Now I feel a little better,
    What a treat to hear Thy Word,
Where the bones of leading statesmen,
    Have so often been interr'd.
And now, dear Lord, I cannot wait
Because I have a luncheon date.

SEAMUS HEANEY 1939–

FOLLOWER

My father worked with a horse-plough,
His shoulders globed like a full sail strung
Between the shafts and the furrow.
The horses strained at his clicking tongue.

An expert. He would set the wing
And fit the bright steel-pointed sock.
The sod rolled over without breaking.
At the headrig, with a single pluck

Of reins, the sweating team turned round
And back into the land. His eye
Narrowed and angled at the ground,
Mapping the furrow exactly.

I stumbled in his hob-nailed wake,
Fell sometimes on the polished sod;
Sometimes he rode me on his back
Dipping and rising to his plod.

I wanted to grow up and plough,
To close one eye, stiffen my arm.
All I ever did was follow
In his broad shadow round the farm.

I was a nuisance, tripping, falling,
Yapping always. But today
It is my father who keeps stumbling
Behind me, and will not go away.

CHARLES CAUSLEY 1917–

TIMOTHY WINTERS

Timothy Winters comes to school
With eyes as wide as a football-pool,
Ears like bombs and teeth like splinters:
A blitz of a boy is Timothy Winters.

His belly is white, his neck is dark,
And his hair is an exclamation-mark.
His clothes are enough to scare a crow
And through his britches the blue winds blow.

When teacher talks he won't hear a word
And he shoots down dead the arithmetic-bird,
He licks the patterns off his plate
And he's not even heard of the Welfare State.

Timothy Winters has bloody feet
And he lives in a house on Suez Street,
He sleeps in a sack on the kitchen floor
And they say there aren't boys like him any more.

Old Man Winters likes his beer
And his missus ran off with a bombardier,
Grandma sits in the grate with a gin
And Timothy's dosed with an aspirin.

The Welfare Worker lies awake
But the law's as tricky as a ten-foot snake,
So Timothy Winters drinks his cup
And slowly goes on growing up.

At Morning Prayers the Master helves
For children less fortunate than ourselves,
And the loudest response in the room is when
Timothy Winters roars 'Amen!'

So come one angel, come on ten:
Timothy Winters says 'Amen
Amen amen amen amen.'
Timothy Winters, Lord.

         Amen.

PHILIP LARKIN 1922–85

THIS BE THE VERSE

They fuck you up, your mum and dad.
  They may not mean to, but they do.
They fill you with the faults they had
  And add some extra, just for you.

But they were fucked up in their turn
  By fools in old-style hats and coats,
Who half the time were soppy-stern
  And half at one another's throats.

Man hands on misery to man.
  It deepens like a coastal shelf.
Get out as early as you can,
  And don't have any kids yourself.

A.E. HOUSMAN 1859–1936

IN VALLEYS GREEN AND STILL

In valleys green and still
  Where lovers wander maying
They hear from over hill
  A music playing.

Behind the drum and fife,
  Past hawthornwood and hollow,
Through earth and out of life
  The soldiers follow.

The soldier's is the trade:
  In any wind or weather
He steals the heart of maid
  And man together.

The lover and his lass
  Beneath the hawthorn lying
Have heard the soldiers pass,
  And both are sighing.

And down the distance they
  With dying note and swelling
Walk the resounding way
  To the still dwelling.

GEORGE MACBETH 1932–92

THE MINER'S HELMET

My father wore it working coal at Shotts
When I was one. My mother stirred his broth
And rocked my cradle with her shivering hands
While this black helmet's long-lost miner's-lamp
Showed him the road home. Through miles of coal
His fragile skull, filled even then with pit-props,
Lay in a shell, the brain's blue-printed future
Warm in its womb. From sheaves of saved brown paper,
Baring an oval into weeks of dust,
I pull it down: its laced straps move to admit
My larger brows; like an abdicated king's
Gold crown of thirty years ago, I touch it
With royal fingers, feel its image firm –
Hands grown to kings' hands calloused on the pick,
Feet slow like kings' feet on the throneward gradient
Up to the coal-face – but the image blurs
Before it settles: there were no crusades.
My father died a draughtsman, drawing plans
In an airy well-lit office above the ground
Beneath which his usurpers, other kings,
Reigned by the fallen helmet he resigned
Which I inherit as a concrete husk.
I hand it back to gather dust on the shelf.

CHARLES CAUSLEY 1917–

BALLAD OF THE BREAD MAN

Mary stood in the kitchen
  Baking a loaf of bread.
An angel flew in through the window.
  'We've a job for you,' he said.

'God in his big gold heaven,
  Sitting in his big blue chair,
Wanted a mother for his little son.
  Suddenly saw you there.'

Mary shook and trembled,
  'It isn't true what you say.'
'Don't say that,' said the angel.
  'The baby's on its way.'

Joseph was in the workshop
  Planing a piece of wood.
'The old man's past it,' the neighbours said.
  'That girl's been up to no good.'

'And who was that elegant fellow,'
  They said, 'in the shiny gear?'
The things they said about Gabriel
  Were hardly fit to hear.

Mary never answered,
  Mary never replied.
She kept the information,
  Like the baby, safe inside.

It was election winter.
  They went to vote in town.
When Mary found her time had come
  The hotels let her down.

The baby was born in an annexe
    Next to the local pub.
At midnight, a delegation
    Turned up from the Farmers' Club.

They talked about an explosion
    That made a hole in the sky,
Said they'd been sent to the Lamb & Flag
    To see God come down from on high.

A few days later a bishop
    And a five-star general were seen
With the head of an African country
    In a bullet-proof limousine.

'We've come,' they said, 'with tokens
    For the little boy to choose.'
Told the tale about war and peace
    In the television news.

After them came the soldiers
    With rifle and bomb and gun,
Looking for enemies of the state.
    The family had packed and gone.

When they got back to the village
    The neighbours said, to a man,
'That boy will never be one of us,
    Though he does what he blessed well can.'

He went round to all the people
    A paper crown on his head.
Here is some bread from my father.
    Take, eat, he said.

Nobody seemed very hungry.
    Nobody seemed to care.
Nobody saw the god in himself
    Quietly standing there.

He finished up in the papers.
    He came to a very bad end.
He was charged with bringing the living to life.
    No man was that prisoner's friend.

There's only one kind of punishment
    To fit that kind of a crime.
They rigged a trial and shot him dead.
    They were only just in time.

They lifted the young man by the leg,
    They lifted him by the arm,
They locked him in a cathedral
    In case he came to harm.

They stored him safe as water
    Under seven rocks.
One Sunday morning he burst out
    Like a jack-in-the-box.

Through the town he went walking.
    He showed them the holes in his head.
Now do you want any loaves? he cried.
    'Not today,' they said.

SIR JOHN BETJEMAN 1906–84

DIARY OF A CHURCH MOUSE

Here among long-discarded cassocks,
Damp stools, and half-split open hassocks,
Here where the Vicar never looks
I nibble through old service books.
Lean and alone I spend my days
Behind this Church of England baize.
I share my dark forgotten room
With two oil-lamps and half a broom.
The cleaner never bothers me,
So here I eat my frugal tea.
My bread is sawdust mixed with straw;
My jam is polish for the floor.
   Christmas and Easter may be feasts
For congregations and for priests,
And so may Whitsun. All the same,
They do not fill my meagre frame.
For me the only feast at all
Is Autumn's Harvest Festival,
When I can satisfy my want
With ears of corn around the font.
I climb the eagle's brazen head
To burrow through a loaf of bread.
I scramble up the pulpit stair
And gnaw the marrows hanging there.
   It is enjoyable to taste
These items ere they go to waste,
But how annoying when one finds
That other mice with pagan minds
Come into church my food to share
Who have no proper business there.
Two field mice who have no desire
To be baptized, invade the choir.
A large and most unfriendly rat

Comes in to see what we are at.
He says he thinks there is no God
And yet he comes . . . it's rather odd.
This year he stole a sheaf of wheat
(It screened our special preacher's seat),
And prosperous mice from fields away
Come in to hear the organ play,
And under cover of its notes
Eat through the altar's sheaf of oats.
A Low Church mouse, who thinks that I
Am too papistical, and High,
Yet somehow doesn't think it wrong
To munch through Harvest Evensong,
While I, who starve the whole year through,
Must share my food with rodents who
Except at this time of the year
Not once inside the church appear.
    Within the human world I know
Such goings-on could not be so,
For human beings only do
What their religion tells them to.
They read the Bible every day
And always, night and morning, pray,
And just like me, the good church mouse,
Worship each week in God's own house,
    But all the same it's strange to me
How very full the church can be
With people I don't see at all
Except at Harvest Festival.

*'Between the streams and the red clouds,
hearing curlews'*

from 'The Horses'

LAURIE LEE 1914–97

APRIL RISE

If ever I saw blessing in the air
    I see it now in this still early day
Where lemon-green the vaporous morning drips
    Wet sunlight on the powder of my eye.

Blown bubble-film of blue, the sky wraps round
    Weeds of warm light whose every root and rod
Splutters with soapy green, and all the world
    Sweats with the bead of summer in its bud.

If ever I heard blessing it is there
    Where birds in trees that shoals and shadows are
Splash with their hidden wings and drops of sound
    Break on my ears their crests of throbbing air.

Pure in the haze the emerald sun dilates,
    The lips of sparrows milk the mossy stones,
While white as water by the lake a girl
    Swims her green hand among the gathered swans.

Now, as the almond burns its smoking wick,
    Dropping small flames to light the candled grass;
Now, as my low blood scales its second chance,
    If ever world were blessed, now it is.

VERNON WATKINS 1906–67

PEACE IN THE WELSH HILLS

Calm is the landscape when the storm has passed,
Brighter the fields, and fresh with fallen rain.
Where gales beat out new colour from the hills
Rivers fly faster, and upon their banks
Birds preen their wings, and irises revive.
Not so the cities burnt alive with fire
Of man's destruction: when their smoke is spent,
No phœnix rises from the ruined walls.

I ponder now the grief of many rooms.
Was it a dream, that age, when fingers found
A satisfaction sleeping in dumb stone,
When walls were built responding to the touch
In whose high gables, in the lengthening days,
Martins would nest? Though crops, though lives, would fail,
Though friends dispersed, unchanged the walls would stay,
And still those wings return to build in Spring.

Here, where the earth is green, where heaven is true
Opening the windows, touched with earliest dawn,
In the first frost of cool September days,
Chrysanthemum weather, presaging great birth,
Who in his heart could murmur or complain:
'The light we look for is not in this land'?
That light is present, and that distant time
Is always here, continually redeemed.

There is a city we must build with joy
Exactly where the fallen city sleeps.
There is one road through village, town and field,
On whose robust foundation Chaucer dreamed
A ride could wed the opposites in man.
There proud walls may endure, and low walls feed
The imagination if they have a vine
Or shadowy barn made rich with gathered corn.

Great mansions fear from their surrounding trees
The invasion of a wintry desolation
Filling their rooms with leaves. And cottages
Bring the sky down as flickering candles do,
Leaning on their own shadows. I have seen
Vases and polished brass reflect black windows
And draw the ceiling down to their vibrations,
Thick, deep, and white-washed, like a bank of snow.

To live entwined in pastoral loveliness
May rest the eyes, throw pictures on the mind,
But most we need a metaphor of stone
Such as those painters had whose mountain-cities
Cast long, low shadows on the Umbrian hills.
There, in some courtyard on the cobbled stone,
A fountain plays, and through a cherub's mouth
Ages are linked by water in the sunlight.

All of good faith that fountain may recall,
Woman, musician, boy, or else a scholar
Reading a Latin book. They seem distinct,
And yet are one, because tranquillity
Affirms the Judgment. So, in these Welsh hills,
I marvel, waking from a dream of stone,
That such a peace surrounds me, while the city
For which all long has never yet been built.

D.H. LAWRENCE 1885–1930

BAVARIAN GENTIANS

Not every man has gentians in his house
in Soft September, at slow, Sad Michaelmas.

Bavarian gentians, big and dark, only dark
darkening the day-time torch-like with the smoking blueness
    of Pluto's gloom,
ribbed and torch-like, with their blaze of darkness spread
    blue
down flattening into points, flattened under the sweep of
    white day
torch-flower of the blue-smoking darkness, Pluto's dark-blue
    daze,
black lamps from the halls of Dis, burning dark blue,
giving off darkness, blue darkness, as Demeter's pale lamps
    give off light,
lead me then, lead me the way.

Reach me a gentian, give me a torch
let me guide myself with the blue, forked torch of this flower
down the darker and darker stairs, where blue is darkened
    on blueness,
even where Persephone goes, just now, from the frosted
    September
to the sightless realm where darkness is awake upon the dark
and Persephone herself is but a voice
or a darkness invisible enfolded in the deeper dark
of the arms Plutonic, and pierced with the passion of dense
    gloom,
among the splendour of torches of darkness, shedding
    darkness on the lost bride and her groom.

R.S. THOMAS 1913–

A PEASANT

Iago Prytherch his name, though, be it allowed,
Just an ordinary man of the bald Welsh hills,
Who pens a few sheep in a gap of cloud.
Docking mangels, chipping the green skin
From the yellow bones with a half-witted grin
Of satisfaction, or churning the crude earth
To a stiff sea of clouds that glint in the wind –
So are his days spent, his spittled mirth
Rarer than the sun that cracks the cheeks
Of the gaunt sky perhaps once in a week.
And then at night see him fixed in his chair
Motionless, except when he leans to gob in the fire.
There is something frightening in the vacancy of his mind.
His clothes, sour with years of sweat
And animal contact, shock the refined,
But affected, sense with their stark naturalness.
Yet this is your prototype, who, season by season
Against siege of rain and the wind's attrition,
Preserves his stock, an impregnable fortress
Not to be stormed even in death's confusion.
Remember him, then, for he, too, is a winner of wars,
Enduring like a tree under the curious stars.

TED HUGHES 1930–98

WIND

This house has been far out at sea all night,
The woods crashing through darkness, the booming hills,
Winds stampeding the fields under the window
Floundering black astride and blinding wet

Till day rose; then under an orange sky
The hills had new places, and wind wielded
Blade-light, luminous black and emerald,
Flexing like the lens of a mad eye.

At noon I scaled along the house-side as far as
The coal-house door. Once I looked up –
Through the brunt wind that dented the balls of my eyes
The tent of the hills drummed and strained its guyrope,

The fields quivering, the skyline a grimace,
At any second to bang and vanish with a flap:
The wind flung a magpie away and a black-
Back gull bent like an iron bar slowly. The house

Rang like some fine green goblet in the note
That any second would shatter it. Now deep
In chairs, in front of the great fire, we grip
Our hearts and cannot entertain book, thought,

Or each other. We watch the fire blazing,
And feel the roots of the house move, but sit on,
Seeing the window tremble to come in,
Hearing the stones cry out under the horizons.

ROBERT FROST 1874–1963

STOPPING BY WOODS ON A SNOWY EVENING

Whose woods these are I think I know.
His house is in the village though;
He will not see me stopping here
To watch his woods fill up with snow.

My little horse must think it queer
To stop without a farmhouse near
Between the woods and frozen lake
The darkest evening of the year.

He gives his harness bells a shake
To ask if there is some mistake.
The only other sound's the sweep
Of easy wind and downy flake.

The woods are lovely, dark and deep.
But I have promises to keep,
And miles to go before I sleep,
And miles to go before I sleep.

TED HUGHES 1930–98

THE HORSES

I climbed through woods in the hour-before-dawn dark.
Evil air, a frost-making stillness,

Not a leaf, not a bird, –
A world cast in frost. I came out above the wood

Where my breath left tortuous statues in the iron light.
But the valleys were draining the darkness

Till the moorline – blackening dregs of the brightening grey –
Halved the sky ahead. And I saw the horses:

Huge in the dense grey – ten together –
Megalith-still. They breathed, making no move,

With draped manes and tilted hind-hooves,
Making no sound.

I passed: not one snorted or jerked its head.
Grey silent fragments

Of a grey silent world.

I listened in emptiness on the moor-ridge.
The curlew's tear turned its edge on the silence.

Slowly detail leafed from the darkness. Then the sun
Orange, red, red erupted.

Silently, and splitting to its core tore and flung cloud,
Shook the gulf open, showed blue,

And the big planets hanging –
I turned

Stumbling in the fever of a dream, down towards
The dark woods, from the kindling tops,

And came to the horses.
                There, still they stood,
But now steaming and glistening under the flow of light,

Their draped stone manes, their tilted hind-hooves
Stirring under a thaw while all around them

The frost showed its fires. But still they made no sound.
Not one snorted or stamped,

Their hung heads patient as the horizons
High over valleys, in the red levelling rays –

In din of the crowded streets, going among the years, the faces,
May I still meet my memory in so lonely a place

Between the streams and the red clouds, hearing curlews,
Hearing the horizons endure.

LAURENCE BINYON 1869–1943

THE BURNING OF THE LEAVES

Now is the time for the burning of the leaves.
They go to the fire; the nostril pricks with smoke
Wandering slowly into the weeping mist.
Brittle and blotched, ragged and rotten sheaves!
A flame seizes the smouldering ruin, and bites
On stubborn stalks that crackle as they resist.

The last hollyhock's fallen tower is dust:
All the spices of June are a bitter reek,
All the extravagant riches spent and mean.
All burns! the reddest rose is a ghost.
Sparks whirl up, to expire in the mist: the wild
Fingers of fire are making corruption clean.

Now is the time for stripping the spirit bare,
Time for the burning of days ended and done,
Idle solace of things that have gone before,
Rootless hope and fruitless desire are there:
Let them go to the fire with never a look behind.
That world that was ours is a world that is ours no more.

They will come again, the leaf and the flower, to arise
From squalor of rottenness into the old splendour,
And magical scents to a wondering memory bring;
The same glory, to shine upon different eyes.
Earth cares for her own ruins, naught for ours.
Nothing is certain, only the certain spring.

'I believe life ends with death, and that is all'

from 'Long Distance II'

ROGER McGOUGH 1937–

LET ME DIE A YOUNGMAN'S DEATH

Let me die a youngman's death
not a clean and inbetween
the sheets holywater death
not a famous-last-words
peaceful out of breath death

When I'm 73
and in constant good tumour
may I be mown down at dawn
by a bright red sports car
on my way home
from an allnight party

Or when I'm 91
with silver hair
and sitting in a barber's chair
may rival gangsters
with hamfisted tommyguns burst in
and give me a short back and insides

Or when I'm 104
and banned from the Cavern
may my mistress
catching me in bed with her daughter
and fearing for her son
cut me up into little pieces
and throw away every piece but one

Let me die a youngman's death
not a free from sin tiptoe in
candle wax and waning death
not a curtains drawn by angels borne
'what a nice way to go' death

JOHN McCRAE 1872–1918

IN FLANDERS FIELDS

In Flanders fields the poppies blow
Between the crosses, row on row,
    That mark our place; and in the sky
    The larks, still bravely singing, fly
Scarce heard amid the guns below.

We are the Dead. Short days ago
We lived, felt dawn, saw sunset glow,
    Loved and were loved, and now we lie
    In Flanders fields.

Take up our quarrel with the foe:
To you from failing hands we throw
    The torch; be yours to hold it high.
    If ye break faith with us who die
We shall not sleep, though poppies grow
    In Flanders fields.

CHARLES CAUSLEY 1917–

I SAW A JOLLY HUNTER

I saw a jolly hunter
  With a jolly gun
Walking in the country
  In the jolly sun.

In the jolly meadow
  Sat a jolly hare.
Saw the jolly hunter.
  Took jolly care.

Hunter jolly eager –
  Sight of jolly prey.
Forgot gun pointing
  Wrong jolly way.

Jolly hunter jolly head
  Over heels gone.
Jolly old safety catch
  Not jolly on.

Bang went the jolly gun.
  Hunter jolly dead.
Jolly hare got clean away.
  Jolly good, I said.

SIR JOHN BETJEMAN 1906–84

DEATH IN LEAMINGTON

She died in the upstairs bedroom
    By the light of the ev'ning star
That shone through the plate glass window
    From over Leamington Spa.

Beside her the lonely crochet
    Lay patiently and unstirred,
But the fingers that would have work'd it
    Were dead as the spoken word.

And Nurse came in with the tea-things
    Breast high 'mid the stands and chairs –
But Nurse was alone with her own little soul,
    And the things were alone with theirs.

She bolted the big round window,
    She let the blinds unroll,
She set a match to the mantle,
    She covered the fire with coal.

And 'Tea!' she said in a tiny voice
    'Wake up! It's nearly *five*.'
Oh! Chintzy, chintzy cheeriness,
    Half dead and half alive!

Do you know that the stucco is peeling?
    Do you know that the heart will stop?
From those yellow Italianate arches
    Do you hear the plaster drop?

Nurse looked at the silent bedstead,
    At the gray, decaying face,
As the calm of a Leamington ev'ning
    Drifted into the place.

She moved the table of bottles
    Away from the bed to the wall,
And tiptoeing gently over the stairs
    Turned down the gas in the hall.

SEAMUS HEANEY 1939–

MID-TERM BREAK

I sat all morning in the college sick bay
Counting bells knelling classes to a close.
At two o'clock our neighbours drove me home.

In the porch I met my father crying –
He had always taken funerals in his stride –
And Big Jim Evans saying it was a hard blow.

The baby cooed and laughed and rocked the pram
When I came in, and I was embarrassed
By old men standing up to shake my hand

And tell me they were 'sorry for my trouble'.
Whispers informed strangers I was the eldest,
Away at school, as my mother held my hand

In hers and coughed out angry tearless sighs.
At ten o'clock the ambulance arrived
With the corpse, stanched and bandaged by the nurses.

Next morning I went up into the room. Snowdrops
And candles soothed the bedside. I saw him
For the first time in six weeks. Paler now,

Wearing a poppy bruise on his left temple,
He lay in the four foot box as in his cot.
No gaudy scars, the bumper knocked him clear.

A four foot box, a foot for every year.

SIEGFRIED SASSOON 1886–1967

THE DEATH-BED

He drowsed and was aware of silence heaped
Round him, unshaken as the steadfast walls;
Aqueous like floating rays of amber light,
Soaring and quivering in the wings of sleep.
Silence and safety; and his mortal shore
Lipped by the inward, moonless waves of death.

Someone was holding water to his mouth.
He swallowed, unresisting; moaned and dropped
Through crimson gloom to darkness; and forgot
The opiate throb and ache that was his wound.
   Water – calm, sliding green above the weir.
   Water – a sky-lit alley for his boat,
   Bird-voiced, and bordered with reflected flowers
   And shaken hues of summer; drifting down,
   He dipped contented oars, and sighed, and slept.

Night, with a gust of wind, was in the ward,
Blowing the curtain to a glimmering curve.
Night. He was blind; he could not see the stars
Glinting among the wraiths of wandering cloud;
Queer blots of colour, purple, scarlet, green,
Flickered and faded in his drowning eyes.

Rain – he could hear it rustling through the dark;
Fragrance and passionless music woven as one;
Warm rain on drooping roses; pattering showers
That soak the woods; not the harsh rain that sweeps
Behind the thunder, but a trickling peace,
Gently and slowly washing life away.

He stirred, shifting his body; then the pain
Leapt like a prowling beast, and gripped and tore
His groping dreams with grinding claws and fangs.
　　But someone was beside him; soon he lay
　　Shuddering because that evil thing had passed.
　　And death, who'd stepped toward him, paused and stared.

Light many lamps and gather round his bed.
Lend him your eyes, warm blood, and will to live.
Speak to him; rouse him; you may save him yet.
He's young; he hated War; how should he die
When cruel old campaigners win safe through?

But death replied: 'I choose him.' So he went,
And there was silence in the summer night;
Silence and safety; and the veils of sleep.
Then, far away, the thudding of the guns.

STEVIE SMITH 1902–71

NOT WAVING BUT DROWNING

Nobody heard him, the dead man,
But still he lay moaning:
I was much further out than you thought
And not waving but drowning.

Poor chap, he always loved larking
And now he's dead
It must have been too cold for him his heart gave way,
They said.

Oh, no no no, it was too cold always
(Still the dead one lay moaning)
I was much too far out all my life
And not waving but drowning.

TED HUGHES 1930–98

VIEW OF A PIG

The pig lay on a barrow dead.
It weighed, they said, as much as three men.
Its eyes closed, pink white eyelashes.
Its trotters stuck straight out.

Such weight and thick pink bulk
Set in death seemed not just dead.
It was less than lifeless, further off.
It was like a sack of wheat.

I thumped it without feeling remorse.
One feels guilty insulting the dead,
Walking on graves. But this pig
Did not seem able to accuse.

It was too dead. Just so much
A poundage of lard and pork.
Its last dignity had entirely gone.
It was not a figure of fun.

Too dead now to pity.
To remember its life, din, stronghold
Of earthly pleasure as it had been,
Seemed a false effort, and off the point.

Too deadly factual. Its weight
Oppressed me – how could it be moved?
And the trouble of cutting it up!
The gash in its throat was shocking, but not pathetic.

Once I ran at a fair in the noise
To catch a greased piglet
That was faster and nimbler than a cat,
Its squeal was the rending of metal.

Pigs must have hot blood, they feel like ovens.
Their bite is worse than a horse's –
They chop a half-moon clean out.
They eat cinders, dead cats.

Distinctions and admirations such
As this one was long finished with.
I stared at it a long time. They were going to scald it,
Scald it and scour it like a doorstep.

PHILIP LARKIN 1922–85

AMBULANCES

Closed like confessionals, they thread
Loud noons of cities, giving back
None of the glances they absorb.
Light glossy grey, arms on a plaque,
They come to rest at any kerb:
All streets in time are visited.

Then children strewn on steps or road,
Or women coming from the shops
Past smells of different dinners, see
A wild white face that overtops
Red stretcher-blankets momently
As it is carried in and stowed,

And sense the solving emptiness
That lies just under all we do,
And for a second get it whole,
So permanent and blank and true.
The fastened doors recede. *Poor soul*,
They whisper at their own distress;

For borne away in deadened air
May go the sudden shut of loss
Round something nearly at an end,
And what cohered in it across
The years, the unique random blend
Of families and fashions, there

At last begin to loosen. Far
From the exchange of love to lie
Unreachable inside a room
The traffic parts to let go by
Brings closer what is left to come,
And dulls to distance all we are.

TONY HARRISON 1937–

LONG DISTANCE II

Though my mother was already two years dead
Dad kept her slippers warming by the gas,
put hot water bottles her side of the bed
and still went to renew her transport pass.

You couldn't just drop in. You had to phone.
He'd put you off an hour to give him time
to clear away her things and look alone
as though his still raw love were such a crime.

He couldn't risk my blight of disbelief
though sure that very soon he'd hear her key
scrape in the rusted lock and end his grief.
He *knew* she'd just popped out to get the tea.

I believe life ends with death, and that is all.
You haven't both gone shopping; just the same,
in my new black leather phone book there's your name
and the disconnected number I still call.

JON SILKIN 1930–
_____

DEATH OF A SON
(*who died in a mental hospital aged one*)

Something has ceased to come along with me.
Something like a person: something very like one.
And there was no nobility in it
Or anything like that.

Something was there like a one year
Old house, dumb as stone. While the near buildings
Sang like birds and laughed
Understanding the pact

They were to have with silence. But he
Neither sang nor laughed. He did not bless silence
Like bread, with words.
He did not forsake silence.

But rather, like a house in mourning
Kept the eye turned in to watch the silence while
The other houses like birds
Sang around him.

And the breathing silence neither
Moved nor was still.

I have seen stones: I have seen brick
But this house was made up of neither bricks nor stone
But a house of flesh and blood
With flesh of stone

And bricks for blood. A house
Of stones and blood in breathing silence with the other
Birds singing crazy on its chimneys.
But this was silence,

This was something else, this was
Hearing and speaking though he was a house drawn
    Into silence, this was
        Something religious in his silence,

    Something shining in his quiet,
This was different this was altogether something else:
    Though he never spoke, this
        Was something to do with death.

    And then slowly the eye stopped looking
Inward. The silence rose and became still.
The look turned to the outer place and stopped,
    With the birds still shrilling around him.
    And as if he could speak

He turned over on his side with his one year
Red as a wound
He turned over as if he could be sorry for this
And out of his eyes two great tears rolled, like stones,
                and he died.

SIEGFRIED SASSOON 1886–1967

BASE DETAILS

If I were fierce, and bald, and short of breath,
　　I'd live with scarlet Majors at the Base,
And speed glum heroes up the line to death.
　　You'd see me with my puffy petulant face,
Guzzling and gulping in the best hotel,
　　Reading the Roll of Honour. 'Poor young chap,'
I'd say – 'I used to know his father well;
　　Yes, we've lost heavily in this last scrap.'
And when the war is done and youth stone dead,
I'd toddle safely home and die – in bed.

WILFRED OWEN 1893–1918

THE SEND-OFF

Down the close, darkening lanes they sang their way
To the siding-shed,
And lined the train with faces grimly gay.

Their breasts were stuck all white with wreath and spray
As men's are, dead.

Dull porters watched them, and a casual tramp
Stood staring hard,
Sorry to miss them from the upland camp.
Then, unmoved, signals nodded, and a lamp
Winked to the guard.

So secretly, like wrongs hushed-up, they went.
They were not ours:
We never heard to which front these were sent.

Nor there if they yet mock what women meant
Who gave them flowers.

Shall they return to beatings of great bells
In wild train-loads?
A few, a few, too few for drums and yells,
May creep back, silent, to still village wells
Up half-known roads.

W.H. AUDEN 1907–73

from TWELVE SONGS

IX

Stop all the clocks, cut off the telephone,
Prevent the dog from barking with a juicy bone,
Silence the pianos and with muffled drum
Bring out the coffin, let the mourners come.

Let aeroplanes circle moaning overhead
Scribbling on the sky the message He Is Dead,
Put crêpe bows round the white necks of the public doves,
Let the traffic policemen wear black cotton gloves.

He was my North, my South, my East and West,
My working week and my Sunday rest,
My noon, my midnight, my talk, my song;
I thought that love would last for ever: I was wrong.

The stars are not wanted now: put out every one;
Pack up the moon and dismantle the sun;
Pour away the ocean and sweep up the wood.
For nothing now can ever come to any good.

'For there is good news yet to hear and fine things to be seen'

from 'The Rolling English Road'

R.S. THOMAS 1913–

THE BRIGHT FIELD

I have seen the sun break through
to illuminate a small field
for a while, and gone my way
and forgotten it. But that was the pearl
of great price, the one field that had
the treasure in it. I realize now
that I must give all that I have
to possess it. Life is not hurrying

on to a receding future, nor hankering after
an imagined past. It is the turning
aside like Moses to the miracle
of the lit bush, to a brightness
that seemed as transitory as your youth
once, but is the eternity that awaits you.

SHEENAGH PUGH 1950–

SOMETIMES

Sometimes things don't go, after all,
from bad to worse. Some years, muscadel
faces down frost; green thrives; the crops don't fail,
sometimes a man aims high, and all goes well.

A people sometimes will step back from war;
elect an honest man; decide they care
enough, that they can't leave some stranger poor.
Some men become what they were born for.

Sometimes our best efforts do not go
amiss; sometimes we do as we meant to.
The sun will sometimes melt a field of sorrow
that seemed hard frozen: may it happen for you.

SIR JOHN BETJEMAN 1906–84

CHRISTMAS

The bells of waiting Advent ring,
   The Tortoise stove is lit again
And lamp-oil light across the night
   Has caught the streaks of winter rain
In many a stained-glass window sheen
From Crimson Lake to Hooker's Green.

The holly in the windy hedge
   And round the Manor House the yew
Will soon be stripped to deck the ledge,
   The altar, font and arch and pew,
So that the villagers can say
'The church looks nice' on Christmas Day.

Provincial public houses blaze
   And Corporation tramcars clang,
On lighted tenements I gaze
   Where paper decorations hang,
And bunting in the red Town Hall
Says 'Merry Christmas to you all.'

And London shops on Christmas Eve
   Are strung with silver bells and flowers
As hurrying clerks the City leave
   To pigeon-haunted classic towers,
And marbled clouds go scudding by
The many-steepled London sky.

And girls in slacks remember Dad,
   And oafish louts remember Mum,
And sleepless children's hearts are glad,
   And Christmas-morning bells say 'Come!'
Even to shining ones who dwell
Safe in the Dorchester Hotel.

And is it true? And is it true,
  This most tremendous tale of all,
Seen in a stained-glass window's hue,
  A Baby in an ox's stall?
The Maker of the stars and sea
Become a Child on earth for me?

And is it true? For if it is,
  No loving fingers tying strings
Around those tissued fripperies,
  The sweet and silly Christmas things,
Bath salts and inexpensive scent
And hideous tie so kindly meant,

No love that in a family dwells,
  No carolling in frosty air,
Nor all the steeple-shaking bells
  Can with this single Truth compare –
That God was Man in Palestine
And lives to-day in Bread and Wine.

PHILIP LARKIN 1922–85

CHURCH GOING

Once I am sure there's nothing going on
I step inside, letting the door thud shut.
Another church: matting, seats, and stone,
And little books; sprawlings of flowers, cut
For Sunday, brownish now; some brass and stuff
Up at the holy end; the small neat organ;
And a tense, musty, unignorable silence,
Brewed God knows how long. Hatless, I take off
My cycle-clips in awkward reverence,

Move forward, run my hand around the font.
From where I stand, the roof looks almost new –
Cleaned, or restored? Someone would know: I don't.
Mounting the lectern, I peruse a few
Hectoring large-scale verses, and pronounce
'Here endeth' much more loudly than I'd meant.
The echoes snigger briefly. Back at the door
I sign the book, donate an Irish sixpence,
Reflect the place was not worth stopping for.

Yet stop I did: in fact I often do,
And always end much at a loss like this,
Wondering what to look for; wondering, too,
When churches fall completely out of use
What we shall turn them into, if we shall keep
A few cathedrals chronically on show,
Their parchment, plate and pyx in locked cases,
And let the rest rent-free to rain and sheep.
Shall we avoid them as unlucky places?

Or, after dark, will dubious women come
To make their children touch a particular stone;
Pick simples for a cancer; or on some
Advised night see walking a dead one?
Power of some sort or other will go on
In games, in riddles, seemingly at random;
But superstition, like belief, must die,
And what remains when disbelief has gone?
Grass, weedy pavement, brambles, buttress, sky,

A shape less recognisable each week,
A purpose more obscure. I wonder who
Will be the last, the very last, to seek
This place for what it was; one of the crew
That tap and jot and know what rood-lofts were?
Some ruin-bibber, randy for antique,
Or Christmas-addict, counting on a whiff
Of gown-and-bands and organ-pipes and myrrh?
Or will he be my representative,

Bored, uninformed, knowing the ghostly silt
Dispersed, yet tending to this cross of ground
Through suburb scrub because it held unspilt
So long and equally what since is found
Only in separation – marriage, and birth,
And death, and thoughts of these – for whom was built
This special shell? For, though I've no idea
What this accoutred frowsty barn is worth,
It pleases me to stand in silence here;

A serious house on serious earth it is,
In whose blent air all our compulsions meet,
Are recognised, and robed as destinies.
And that much never can be obsolete,
Since someone will forever be surprising
A hunger in himself to be more serious,
And gravitating with it to this ground,
Which, he once heard, was proper to grow wise in,
If only that so many dead lie round.

CAROL ANN DUFFY 1955–

PRAYER

Some days, although we cannot pray, a prayer
utters itself. So, a woman will lift
her head from the sieve of her hands and stare
at the minims sung by a tree, a sudden gift.

Some nights, although we are faithless, the truth
enters our hearts, that small familiar pain;
then a man will stand stock-still, hearing his youth
in the distant Latin chanting of a train.

Pray for us now. Grade I piano scales
console the lodger looking out across
a Midlands town. Then dusk, and someone calls
a child's name as though they named their loss.

Darkness outside. Inside, the radio's prayer –
Rockall. Malin. Dogger. Finisterre.

W.B. YEATS 1865–1939

SAILING TO BYZANTIUM

I

That is no country for old men. The young
In one another's arms, birds in the trees
– Those dying generations – at their song,
The salmon-falls, the mackerel-crowded seas,
Fish, flesh, or fowl, commend all summer long
Whatever is begotten, born, and dies.
Caught in that sensual music all neglect
Monuments of unageing intellect.

II

An aged man is but a paltry thing,
A tattered coat upon a stick, unless
Soul clap its hands and sing, and louder sing
For every tatter in its mortal dress,
Nor is there singing school but studying
Monuments of its own magnificence;
And therefore I have sailed the seas and come
To the holy city of Byzantium.

III

O sages standing in God's holy fire
As in the gold mosaic of a wall,
Come from the holy fire, perne in a gyre,
And be the singing-masters of my soul.
Consume my heart away; sick with desire
And fastened to a dying animal
It knows not what it is; and gather me
Into the artifice of eternity.

IV

Once out of nature I shall never take
My bodily form from any natural thing,
But such a form as Grecian goldsmiths make
Of hammered gold and gold enamelling
To keep a drowsy Emperor awake;
Or set upon a golden bough to sing
To lords and ladies of Byzantium
Of what is past, or passing, or to come.

TED HUGHES 1930–98

THE THOUGHT-FOX

I imagine this midnight moment's forest:
Something else is alive
Beside the clock's loneliness
And this blank page where my fingers move.

Through the window I see no star:
Something more near
Though deeper within darkness
Is entering the loneliness:

Cold, delicately as the dark snow
A fox's nose touches twig, leaf;
Two eyes serve a movement, that now
And again now, and now, and now

Sets neat prints into the snow
Between trees, and warily a lame
Shadow lags by stump and in hollow
Of a body that is bold to come

Across clearings, an eye,
A widening deepening greenness,
Brilliantly, concentratedly,
Coming about its own business

Till with a sudden sharp hot stink of fox
It enters the dark hole of the head.
The window is starless still; the clock ticks,
The page is printed.

BENJAMIN ZEPHANIAH 1958–

DIS POETRY

Dis poetry is like a riddim dat drops
De tongue fires a riddim dat shoots like shots
Dis poetry is designed fe rantin
Dance hall style, Big mouth chanting,
Dis poetry nar put yu to sleep
Preaching follow me
Like yu is blind sheep,
Dis poetry is not Party Political
Not designed fe dose who are critical.

Dis poetry is wid me when I gu to me bed
It gets into me Dreadlocks
It lingers around me head
Dis poetry goes wid me as I pedal me bike
I've tried Shakespeare, Respect due dere
But dis is de stuff I like

Dis poetry is not afraid of going ina book
Still dis poetry need ears fe hear an eyes fe hav a look
Dis poetry is Verbal Riddim, no big words involved
An if I hav a problem de riddim gets it solved,
I've tried to be more Romantic, it does nu good for me
So I tek a Reggae Riddim an build me poetry,
I could try be more personal
But you've heard it all before,
Pages of written words no needed
Brain has many words in store,
Yu could call dis poetry Dub Ranting
De tongue plays a beat
De body starts skanking,
Dis poetry is quick an childish
Dis poetry is fe de wise an foolish
Anybody can do it fe free,

Dis poetry is fe yu an me,
Don't stretch yu imagination
Dis poetry is fe de good of de Nation,
Chant,
In de morning
I chant
In de night
I chant
In de darkness
An under de spotlight,
I pass thru University
I pass thru Sociology
An den I got a Dread degree
In Dreadfull Ghettology.

Dis poetry stays wid me when I run or walk
An when I am talking to meself in poetry I talk,
Dis poetry is wid me,
Below me an above,
Dis poetry's from inside me
It goes to yu
WID LUV.

SEAMUS HEANEY 1939–

DIGGING

Between my finger and my thumb
The squat pen rests; snug as a gun.

Under my window, a clean rasping sound
When the spade sinks into gravelly ground:
My father, digging. I look down

Till his straining rump among the flowerbeds
Bends low, comes up twenty years away
Stooping in rhythm through potato drills
Where he was digging.

The coarse boot nestled on the lug, the shaft
Against the inside knee was levered firmly.
He rooted out tall tops, buried the bright edge deep
To scatter new potatoes that we picked
Loving their cool hardness in our hands.

By God, the old man could handle a spade.
Just like his old man.

My grandfather cut more turf in a day
Than any other man on Toner's bog.
Once I carried him milk in a bottle
Corked sloppily with paper. He straightened up
To drink it, then fell to right away
Nicking and slicing neatly, heaving sods
Over his shoulder, going down and down
For the good turf. Digging.

The cold smell of potato mould, the squelch and slap
Of soggy peat, the curt cuts of an edge
Through living roots awaken in my head.
But I've no spade to follow men like them.

Between my finger and my thumb
The squat pen rests.
I'll dig with it.

T.S. ELIOT 1885–1965

---

from LITTLE GIDDING

I

Midwinter spring is its own season
Sempiternal though sodden towards sundown,
Suspended in time, between pole and tropic.
When the short day is brightest, with frost and fire,
The brief sun flames the ice, on pond and ditches,
In windless cold that is the heart's heat,
Reflecting in a watery mirror
A glare that is blindness in the early afternoon.
And glow more intense than blaze of branch, or brazier,
Stirs the dumb spirit: no wind, but pentecostal fire
In the dark time of the year. Between melting and freezing
The soul's sap quivers. There is no earth smell
Or smell of living thing. This is the spring time
But not in time's covenant. Now the hedgerow
Is blanched for an hour with transitory blossom
Of snow, a bloom more sudden
Than that of summer, neither budding nor fading,
Not in the scheme of generation.
Where is the summer, the unimaginable
Zero summer?

If you came this way,
Taking the route you would be likely to take
From the place you would be likely to come from,
If you came this way in may time, you would find the hedges
White again, in May, with voluptuary sweetness.
It would be the same at the end of the journey,
If you came at night like a broken king,

If you came by day not knowing what you came for,
It would be the same, when you leave the rough road
And turn behind the pig-sty to the dull façade
And the tombstone. And what you thought you came for
Is only a shell, a husk of meaning
From which the purpose breaks only when it is fulfilled
If at all. Either you had no purpose
Or the purpose is beyond the end you figured
And is altered in fulfilment. There are other places
Which also are the world's end, some at the sea jaws,
Or over a dark lake, in a desert or a city –
But this is the nearest, in place and time,
Now and in England.

                  If you came this way,
Taking any route, starting from anywhere,
At any time or at any season,
It would always be the same: you would have to put off
Sense and notion. You are not here to verify,
Instruct yourself, or inform curiosity
Or carry report. You are here to kneel
Where prayer has been valid. And prayer is more
Than an order of words, the conscious occupation
Of the praying mind, or the sound of the voice praying.
And what the dead had no speech for, when living,
They can tell you, being dead: the communication
Of the dead is tongued with fire beyond the language of the living.
Here, the intersection of the timeless moment
Is England and nowhere. Never and always.

G.K. CHESTERTON 1874–1936

THE ROLLING ENGLISH ROAD

Before the Roman came to Rye or out to Severn strode,
The rolling English drunkard made the rolling English road.
A reeling road, a rolling road, that rambles round the shire,
And after him the parson ran, the sexton and the squire;
A merry road, a mazy road, and such as we did tread
The night we went to Birmingham by way of Beachy Head.

I knew no harm of Bonaparte and plenty of the Squire,
And for to fight the Frenchman I did not much desire;
But I did bash their baggonets because they came arrayed
To straighten out the crooked road an English drunkard made,
Where you and I went down the lane with ale-mugs in our hands,
The night we went to Glastonbury by way of Goodwin Sands.

His sins they were forgiven him; or why do flowers run
Behind him; and the hedges all strengthening in the sun?
The wild thing went from left to right and knew not which was which,
But the wild rose was above him when they found him in the ditch.
God pardon us, nor harden us; we did not see so clear
The night we went to Bannockburn by way of Brighton Pier.

My friends, we will not go again or ape an ancient rage,
Or stretch the folly of our youth to be the shame of age,
But walk with clearer eyes and ears this path that wandereth,
And see undrugged in evening light the decent inn of death;
For there is good news yet to hear and fine things to be seen
Before we go to Paradise by way of Kensal Green.

LAURIE LEE 1914–97

CHRISTMAS LANDSCAPE

To-night the wind gnaws
with teeth of glass,
the jackdaw shivers
in caged branches of iron,
the stars have talons.

There is hunger in the mouth
of vole and badger,
silver agonies of breath
in the nostril of the fox,
ice on the rabbit's paw.

Tonight has no moon,
no food for the pilgrim;
the fruit tree is bare,
the rose bush a thorn
and the ground bitter with stones.

But the mole sleeps, and the hedgehog
lies curled in a womb of leaves,
the bean and the wheat-seed
hug their germs in the earth
and the stream moves under the ice.

Tonight there is no moon,
but a new star opens
like a silver trumpet over the dead.
Tonight in a nest of ruins
the blessed babe is laid.

And the fir tree warms to a bloom of candles,
the child lights his lantern,
stares at his tinselled toy;
our hearts and hearths
smoulder with live ashes.

In the blood of our grief
the cold earth is suckled,
in our agony the womb
convulses its seed,
in the cry of anguish
the child's first breath is born.

STEPHEN SPENDER 1909–95

I THINK CONTINUALLY OF THOSE WHO WERE TRULY GREAT

I think continually of those who were truly great.
Who, from the womb, remembered the soul's history
Through corridors of light where the hours are suns,
Endless and singing. Whose lovely ambition
Was that their lips, still touched with fire,
Should tell of the Spirit, clothed from head to foot in song.
And who hoarded from the Spring branches
The desires falling across their bodies like blossoms.

What is precious is never to forget
The essential delight of the blood drawn from ageless springs
Breaking through rocks in worlds before our earth.
Never to deny its pleasure in the morning simple light
Nor its grave evening demand for love.
Never to allow gradually the traffic to smother
With noise and fog, the flowering of the Spirit.

Near the snow, near the sun, in the highest fields,
See how these names are fêted by the waving grass
And by the streamers of white cloud
And whispers of wind in the listening sky.
The names of those who in their lives fought for life,
Who wore at their hearts the fire's centre.
Born of the sun, they travelled a short while toward the sun
And left the vivid air signed with their honour.

'Time held me green and dying'

from 'Fern Hill'

DYLAN THOMAS 1914–53

FERN HILL

Now as I was young and easy under the apple boughs
About the lilting house and happy as the grass was green,
   The night above the dingle starry,
     Time let me hail and climb
   Golden in the heydays of his eyes,
And honoured among wagons I was prince of the apple towns
And once below a time I lordly had the trees and leaves
     Trail with daisies and barley
   Down the rivers of the windfall light.

And as I was green and carefree, famous among the barns
About the happy yard and singing as the farm was home,
   In the sun that is young once only,
     Time let me play and be
   Golden in the mercy of his means,
And green and golden I was huntsman and herdsman, the calves
Sang to my horn, the foxes on the hills barked clear and cold,
     And the sabbath rang slowly
   In the pebbles of the holy streams.

All the sun long it was running, it was lovely, the hay
Fields high as the house, the tunes from the chimneys, it was air
   And playing, lovely and watery
     And fire green as grass.
   And nightly under the simple stars
As I rode to sleep the owls were bearing the farm away,
All the moon long I heard, blessed among stables, the nightjars
     Flying with the ricks, and the horses
       Flashing into the dark.

And then to awake, and the farm, like a wanderer white
With the dew, come back, the cock on his shoulder: it was all
    Shining, it was Adam and maiden,
       The sky gathered again
    And the sun grew round that very day.
So it must have been after the birth of the simple light
In the first, spinning place, the spellbound horses walking warm
    Out of the whinnying green stable
       On to the fields of praise.

And honoured among foxes and pheasants by the gay house
Under the new made clouds and happy as the heart was long,
    In the sun born over and over,
       I ran my heedless ways,
    My wishes raced through the house high hay
And nothing I cared, at my sky blue trades, that time allows
In all his tuneful turning so few and such morning songs
    Before the children green and golden
       Follow him out of grace,

Nothing I cared, in the lamb white days, that time would take me
Up to the swallow thronged loft by the shadow of my hand,
    In the moon that is always rising,
       Nor that riding to sleep
    I should hear him fly with the high fields
And wake to the farm forever fled from the childless land.
Oh as I was young and easy in the mercy of his means,
       Time held me green and dying
    Though I sang in my chains like the sea.

SEAMUS HEANEY 1939–

BLACKBERRY-PICKING
For Philip Hobsbaum

Late August, given heavy rain and sun
For a full week, the blackberries would ripen.
At first, just one, a glossy purple clot
Among others, red, green, hard as a knot.
You ate that first one and its flesh was sweet
Like thickened wine: summer's blood was in it
Leaving stains upon the tongue and lust for
Picking. Then red ones inked up and that hunger
Sent us out with milk-cans, pea-tins, jam-pots
Where briars scratched and wet grass bleached our boots.
Round hayfields, cornfields and potato-drills
We trekked and picked until the cans were full,
Until the tinkling bottom had been covered
With green ones, and on top big dark blobs burned
Like a plate of eyes. Our hands were peppered
With thorn pricks, our palms sticky as Bluebeard's.

We hoarded the fresh berries in the byre.
But when the bath was filled we found a fur,
A rat-grey fungus, glutting on our cache.
The juice was stinking too. Once off the bush
The fruit fermented, the sweet flesh would turn sour.
I always felt like crying. It wasn't fair
That all the lovely canfuls smelt of rot.
Each year I hoped they'd keep, knew they would not.

THOMAS HARDY 1840–1928

'IF IT'S EVER SPRING AGAIN'

If it's ever spring again,
    Spring again,
I shall go where went I when
Down the moor-cock splashed, and hen,
Seeing me not, amid their flounder,
Standing with my arm around her;
If it's ever spring again,
    Spring again,
I shall go where went I then.

If it's ever summer-time,
    Summer-time,
With the hay crop at the prime,
And the cuckoos – two – in rhyme,
As they used to be, or seemed to,
We shall do as long we've dreamed to,
If it's ever summer-time,
    Summer-time,
With the hay, and bees achime.

DYLAN THOMAS 1914–53

THE FORCE THAT THROUGH THE GREEN FUSE DRIVES THE FLOWER

The force that through the green fuse drives the flower
Drives my green age; that blasts the roots of trees
Is my destroyer.
And I am dumb to tell the crooked rose
My youth is bent by the same wintry fever.

The force that drives the water through the rocks
Drives my red blood; that dries the mouthing streams
Turns mine to wax.
And I am dumb to mouth unto my veins
How at the mountain spring the same mouth sucks.

The hand that whirls the water in the pool
Stirs the quicksand; that ropes the blowing wind
Hauls my shroud sail.
And I am dumb to tell the hanging man
How of my clay is made the hangman's lime.

The lips of time leech to the fountain head;
Love drips and gathers, but the fallen blood
Shall calm her sores.
And I am dumb to tell a weather's wind
How time has ticked a heaven round the stars.

And I am dumb to tell the lover's tomb
How at my sheet goes the same crooked worm.

GAVIN EWART 1916–95

A 14-YEAR-OLD CONVALESCENT CAT IN THE WINTER

I want him to have another living summer,
to lie in the sun and enjoy the *douceur de vivre* –
because the sun, like golden rum in a rummer,
is what makes an idle cat *un tout petit peu ivre* –

I want him to lie stretched out, contented,
revelling in the heat, his fur all dry and warm,
an Old Age Pensioner, retired, resented
by no one, and happinesses in a beelike swarm

to settle on him – postponed for another season
that last fated hateful journey to the vet
from which there is no return (and age the reason),
which must soon come – as I cannot forget.

DYLAN THOMAS 1914–53

POEM IN OCTOBER

It was my thirtieth year to heaven
Woke to my hearing from harbour and neighbour wood
And the mussel pooled and the heron
Priested shore
The morning beckon
With water praying and call of seagull and rook
And the knock of sailing boats on the net webbed wall
Myself to set foot
That second
In the still sleeping town and set forth.

My birthday began with the water-
Birds and the birds of the winged trees flying my name
Above the farms and the white horses
And I rose
In rainy autumn
And walked abroad in a shower of all my days.
High tide and the heron dived when I took the road
Over the border
And the gates
Of the town closed as the town awoke.

A springful of larks in a rolling
Cloud and the roadside bushes brimming with whistling
Blackbirds and the sun of October
Summery
On the hill's shoulder,
Here were fond climates and sweet singers suddenly
Come in the morning where I wandered and listened
To the rain wringing
Wind blow cold
In the wood faraway under me.

Pale rain over the dwindling harbour
And over the sea wet church the size of a snail
  With its horns through mist and the castle
    Brown as owls
   But all the gardens
Of spring and summer were blooming in the tall tales
Beyond the border and under the lark full cloud.
    There could I marvel
     My birthday
Away but the weather turned around.

  It turned away from the blithe country
And down the other air and the blue altered sky
  Streamed again a wonder of summer
    With apples
   Pears and red currants
And I saw in the turning so clearly a child's
Forgotten mornings when he walked with his mother
    Through the parables
     Of sunlight
And the legends of the green chapels

  And the twice told fields of infancy
That his tears burned my cheeks and his heart moved in mine.
  These were the woods the river and sea
    Where a boy
   In the listening
Summertime of the dead whispered the truth of his joy
To the trees and the stones and the fish in the tide.
    And the mystery
     Sang alive
Still in the water and singingbirds.

And there could I marvel my birthday
Away but the weather turned around. And the true
Joy of the long dead child sang burning
In the sun.
It was my thirtieth
Year to heaven stood there then in the summer noon
Though the town below lay leaved with October blood.
O may my heart's truth
Still be sung
On this high hill in a year's turning.

A.E. HOUSMAN 1859–1936

INTO MY HEART AN AIR THAT KILLS

Into my heart an air that kills
From yon far country blows:
What are those blue remembered hills,
What spires, what farms are those?

That is the land of lost content,
I see it shining plain,
The happy highways where I went
And cannot come again.

*'Things fall apart; the centre cannot hold;
Mere anarchy is loosed upon the world'*

from 'The Second Coming'

EDWIN MUIR 1887–1959

THE HORSES

Barely a twelvemonth after
The seven days war that put the world to sleep,
Late in the evening the strange horses came.
By then we had made our covenant with silence,
But in the first few days it was so still
We listened to our breathing and were afraid.
On the second day
The radios failed; we turned the knobs; no answer.
On the third day a warship passed us, heading north,
Dead bodies piled on the deck. On the sixth day
A plane plunged over us into the sea. Thereafter
Nothing. The radios dumb;
And still they stand in corners of our kitchens,
And stand, perhaps, turned on, in a million rooms
All over the world. But now if they should speak,
If on a sudden they should speak again,
If on the stroke of noon a voice should speak,
We would not listen, we would not let it bring
That old bad world that swallowed its children quick
At one great gulp. We would not have it again.
Sometimes we think of the nations lying asleep,
Curled blindly in impenetrable sorrow,
And then the thought confounds us with its strangeness.
The tractors lie about our fields; at evening
They look like dank sea-monsters couched and waiting.
We leave them where they are and let them rust:
'They'll moulder away and be like other loam'.
We make our oxen drag our rusty ploughs,
Long laid aside. We have gone back
Far past our fathers' land.
                    And then, that evening
Late in the summer the strange horses came.
We heard a distant tapping on the road,

A deepening drumming; it stopped, went on again
And at the corner changed to hollow thunder.
We saw the heads
Like a wild wave charging and were afraid.
We had sold our horses in our fathers' time
To buy new tractors. Now they were strange to us
As fabulous steeds set on an ancient shield
Or illustrations in a book of knights.
We did not dare go near them. Yet they waited,
Stubborn and shy, as if they had been sent
By an old command to find our whereabouts
And that long-lost archaic companionship.
In the first moment we had never a thought
That they were creatures to be owned and used.
Among them were some half-a-dozen colts
Dropped in some wilderness of the broken world,
Yet new as if they had come from their own Eden.
Since then they have pulled our ploughs and borne our loads,
But that free servitude still can pierce our hearts.
Our life is changed; their coming our beginning.

ROGER McGOUGH 1937–

AT LUNCHTIME

When the bus stopped suddenly
to avoid damaging
a mother and child in the road,
the younglady in the green hat sitting opposite,
was thrown across me,
and not being one to miss an opportunity
i started to make love.

At first, she resisted,
saying that it was too early in the morning,
and too soon after breakfast,
and anyway, she found me repulsive.
But when i explained
that this being a nuclearage
the world was going to end at lunchtime,
she took off her green hat,
put her busticket into her pocket
and joined in the exercise.

The buspeople,
and there were many of them,
were shockedandsurprised,
and amusedandannoyed.
But when word got around
that the world was going to end at lunchtime,
they put their pride in their pockets
with their bustickets
and made love one with the other.
And even the busconductor,
feeling left out,
climbed into the cab,
and struck up some sort of relationship with the driver.

That night,
on the bus coming home,
we were all a little embarrassed.
Especially me and the younglady in the green hat.
And we all started to say
in different ways
how hasty and foolish we had been.
But then, always having been a bitofalad,
i stood up and said it was a pity
that the world didnt nearly end every lunchtime,
and that we could always pretend.
And then it happened . . .

Quick asa crash
we all changed partners,
and soon the bus was aquiver
with white, mothball bodies doing naughty things.

And the next day
and everyday
In everybus
In everystreet
In everytown
In everycountry

People pretended
that the world was coming to an end at lunchtime.
It still hasnt.
Although in a way it has.

WALTER DE LA MARE 1873–1956

THE LISTENERS

'Is there anybody there?' said the Traveller,
　　Knocking on the moonlit door;
And his horse in the silence champed the grasses
　　Of the forest's ferny floor:
And a bird flew up out of the turret,
　　Above the Traveller's head:
And he smote upon the door again a second time;
　　'Is there anybody there?' he said.
But no one descended to the Traveller;
　　No head from the leaf-fringed sill
Leaned over and looked into his grey eyes,
　　Where he stood perplexed and still.
But only a host of phantom listeners
　　That dwelt in the lone house then
Stood listening in the quiet of the moonlight
　　To that voice from the world of men:
Stood thronging the faint moonbeams on the dark stair,
　　That goes down to the empty hall,
Harkening in an air stirred and shaken
　　By the lonely Traveller's call.
And he felt in his heart their strangeness,
　　Their stillness answering his cry,
While his horse moved, cropping the dark turf,
　　'Neath the starred and leafy sky;
For he suddenly smote on the door, even
　　Louder, and lifted his head: –

'Tell them I came, and no one answered,
    That I kept my word,' he said.
Never the least stir made the listeners,
    Though every word he spake
Fell echoing through the shadowiness of the still house
    From the one man left awake:
Ay, they heard his foot upon the stirrup,
    And the sound of iron on stone,
And how the silence surged softly backward,
When the plunging hoofs were gone.

ADRIAN MITCHELL 1932–

FIFTEEN MILLION PLASTIC BAGS

I was walking in a government warehouse
Where the daylight never goes.
I saw fifteen million plastic bags
Hanging in a thousand rows.

Five million bags were six feet long
Five million bags were five foot five
Five million were stamped with Mickey Mouse
And they came in a smaller size.

Were they for guns or uniforms
Or a dirty kind of party game?
Then I saw each bag had a number
And every bag bore a name.

And five million bags were six feet long
Five million were five foot five
Five million were stamped with Mickey Mouse
And they came in a smaller size

So I've taken my bag from the hanger
And I've pulled it over my head
And I'll wait for the priest to zip it
So the radiation won't spread

Now five million bags are six feet long
Five million are five foot five
Five million are stamped with Mickey Mouse
And they come in a smaller size.

T.S. ELIOT 1885–1965

---

from THE WASTE LAND

II. A Game of Chess

The Chair she sat in, like a burnished throne,
Glowed on the marble, where the glass
Held up by standards wrought with fruited vines
From which a golden Cupidon peeped out
(Another hid his eyes behind his wing)
Doubled the flames of sevenbranched candelabra
Reflecting light upon the table as
The glitter of her jewels rose to meet it,
From satin cases poured in rich profusion;
In vials of ivory and coloured glass
Unstoppered, lurked her strange synthetic perfumes,
Unguent, powdered, or liquid – troubled, confused
And drowned the sense in odours; stirred by the air
That freshened from the window, these ascended
In fattening the prolonged candle-flames,
Flung their smoke into the laqueraria,
Stirring the pattern on the coffered ceiling.
Huge sea-wood fed with copper
Burned green and orange, framed by the coloured stone,
In which sad light a carved dolphin swam.
Above the antique mantel was displayed
As though a window gave upon the sylvan scene
The change of Philomel, by the barbarous king
So rudely forced; yet there the nightingale
Filled all the desert with inviolable voice
And still she cried, and still the world pursues,
"Jug Jug" to dirty ears.
And other withered stumps of time
Were told upon the walls; staring forms
Leaned out, leaning, hushing the room enclosed.
Footsteps shuffled on the stair.
Under the firelight, under the brush, her hair
  Spread out in fiery points

Glowed into words, then would be savagely still.
"My nerves are bad to-night. Yes, bad. Stay with me.
"Speak to me. Why do you never speak. Speak.
   "What are you thinking of? What thinking? What?
"I never know what you are thinking. Think."

I think we are in rats' alley
Where the dead men lost their bones.

"What is that noise?"
                              The wind under the door.
"What is that noise now? What is the wind doing?"
                              Nothing again Nothing.
                                        "Do
"You know nothing? Do you see nothing? Do you remember
"Nothing?"
   I remember
Those are pearls that were his eyes.
"Are you alive, or not? Is there nothing in your head?"
                                                  But

O O O O that Shakespeherian Rag –
It's so elegant
So intelligent
"What shall I do now? What shall I do?"
"I shall rush out as I am, and walk the street
"With my hair down, so. What shall we do tomorrow?
"What shall we ever do?"
                              The hot water at ten.
And if it rains, a closed car at four.
And we shall play a game of chess,
Pressing lidless eyes and waiting for a knock upon the door.

When Lil's husband got demobbed, I said –
I didn't mince my words, I said to her myself,

HURRY UP PLEASE ITS TIME
Now Albert's coming back, make yourself a bit smart.
He'll want to know what you done with that money he gave you
To get yourself some teeth. He did, I was there.
You have them all out, Lil, and get a nice set,
He said, I swear, I can't bear to look at you.
And no more can't I, I said, and think of poor Albert,
He's been in the army four years, he wants a good time,
And if you don't give it him, there's others will, I said.
Oh is there, she said. Something o' that, I said.
Then I'll know who to thank, she said, and give me a straight look.
HURRY UP PLEASE ITS TIME
If you don't like it you can get on with it, I said,
Others can pick and choose if you can't.
But if Albert makes off, it won't be for lack of telling.
You ought to be ashamed, I said, to look so antique.
(And her only thirty-one.)
I can't help it, she said, pulling a long face,
It's them pills I took, to bring it off, she said.
(She's had five already, and nearly died of young George.)
The chemist said it would be all right, but I've never been the same.
You *are* a proper fool I said.
Well, if Albert won't leave you alone, there it is, I said,
What you get married for if you don't want children?
HURRY UP PLEASE ITS TIME
Well, that Sunday Albert was home, they had a hot gammon,
And they asked me in to dinner, to get the beauty of it hot –
HURRY UP PLEASE ITS TIME
HURRY UP PLEASE ITS TIME
Goodnight Bill. Goodnight Lou. Goodnight May. Goodnight.
Ta ta. Goodnight. Goodnight.
Good night, ladies, good night, sweet ladies, good night,
 good night.

W.B. YEATS 1865–1939

THE SECOND COMING

Turning and turning in the widening gyre
The falcon cannot hear the falconer;
Things fall apart; the centre cannot hold;
Mere anarchy is loosed upon the world,
The blood-dimmed tide is loosed, and everywhere
The ceremony of innocence is drowned;
The best lack all conviction, while the worst
Are full of passionate intensity.

Surely some revelation is at hand;
Surely the Second Coming is at hand.
The Second Coming! Hardly are those words out
When a vast image out of *Spiritus Mundi*
Troubles my sight: somewhere in sands of the desert
A shape with lion body and the head of a man,
A gaze blank and pitiless as the sun,
Is moving its slow thighs, while all about it
Reel shadows of the indignant desert birds.
The darkness drops again; but now I know
That twenty centuries of stony sleep
Were vexed to nightmare by a rocking cradle,
And what rough beast, its hour come round at last,
Slouches towards Bethlehem to be born?

ACKNOWLEDGEMENTS

— ◇ —

The publishers would like to acknowledge the following for permission to reproduce copyright material. Every effort has been made to trace copyright holders but in a few cases this has proved impossible. The publishers would be interested to hear from any copyright holders not here acknowledged.

14. 'What If' was first commissioned by the BBC for National Poetry Day. Copyright © Benjamin Zephaniah 1996.

15. A.P. Watt on behalf of The National Trust for Places of Historic Interest or Natural Beauty for 'If—' from *Rudyard Kipling's Verse: Definitive Edition*.

19, 167, 171, 173. 'Do not go gentle into that good night', 'Fern Hill', 'The force that through the green fuse drives the flower' and 'Poem in October' from *The Collected Poems* by Dylan Thomas, published by J.M. Dent. Reprinted by permission of David Higham Associates.

20. 'Warning' from *Selected Poems* by Jenny Joseph, published by Bloodaxe Books (1992). Reprinted by permission of John Johnson Ltd.

21. 'The Midnight Skaters' from *Poems 1914–1930* by Edmund Blunden, published by Macmillan. Reprinted by permission of The Peters Fraser and Dunlop Group.

22, 30. Faber and Faber Ltd for 'Lady Lazarus' and 'Daddy' from *Collected Poems* by Sylvia Plath.

26, 62, 151, 189. A.P. Watt on behalf of Michael Yeats for 'An Irish Airman Foresees His Death', 'He Wishes for the Cloths of Heaven', 'Sailing to Byzantium' and 'The Second Coming' from *The Collected Poems of W.B. Yeats*.

27, 35. 'Phenomenal Woman' and 'Still I Rise' from *And Still I Rise* by Maya Angelou. Copyright © 1978 by Maya Angelou. Reprinted by permission of Virago Press and Random House, Inc.

33. 'Autumn Verses' is from *Love Cuts* by John Hegley, published by Methuen, London (1995). Copyright © John Hegley 1995.

34. 'My Old Cat' by Hal Summers is reprinted by permission of the author.

39, 83, 87, 100, 134. Faber and Faber Ltd for 'An Arundel Tomb', 'Going, Going', 'The Whitsun Weddings', 'This Be the Verse' and 'Ambulances' from *Collected Poems* by Philip Larkin.

41. 'somewhere I have never travelled,gladly beyond' is reprinted from *Complete Poems 1904–1962*, by E.E. Cummings, edited by George J. Firmage, by permission of W.W. Norton & Company. Copyright © 1991 by the Trustees for the E.E. Cummings Trust and George James Firmage.

42, 61, 90, 95, 106, 126, 145. John Murray for 'A Subaltern's Love-song', 'Myfanwy', 'Slough', 'In Westminster Abbey', 'Diary of a Church Mouse', 'Death in Leamington' and 'Christmas' from *Collected Poems* by John Betjeman.

44, 81, 140. Faber and Faber Ltd for 'Carry Her Over the Water', 'Night Mail' and 'Stop all the clocks' (IX from Twelve Songs) from *Collected Poems* by W.H. Auden.

45. 'The Almond Tree' from *Root and Branch* by Jon Stallworthy, published by Chatto & Windus.

50. 'Meeting Point' from *Collected Poems* by Louis MacNeice, published by Faber and Faber Ltd. Reprinted by permission of David Higham Associates.

52. 'Without You' from *Collected Poems* by Adrian Henri, published by Allison & Busby (1986). Copyright © Adrian Henri 1986. Reproduced by permission of the author c/o Rogers, Coleridge & White Ltd, 20 Powis Mews, London W11 1JN.

55. Extract from *Under Milk Wood* by Dylan Thomas, published by J.M. Dent. Reprinted by permission of David Higham Associates.

58, 131. James MacGibbon for 'The Singing Cat' and 'Not Waving but Drowning' from *The Collected Poems of Stevie Smith* (Penguin Twentieth Century Classics).

59. Carcanet Press for 'Strawberries' from *Collected Poems* (1990) by Edwin Morgan.

60, 67, 181. 'Vinegar', 'Comeclose and Sleepnow' and 'At Lunchtime' from *Blazing Fruit* by Roger McGough. Reprinted by permission of The Peters Fraser and Dunlop Group on behalf of Roger McGough.

65. 'Tides' is from *Love Life* by Hugo Williams. Reprinted by permission of the author.

66, 74. Faber and Faber Ltd for 'Loss' and 'A Christmas Poem' from *Serious Concerns* by Wendy Cope.

68. 'Portrait of a Young Girl Raped at a Suburban Party' from *Notes to the Hurrying Man* by Brian Patten, published by George Allen and Unwin Ltd (1969). Copyright © Brian Patten 1969. Reproduced by permission of the author c/o Rogers, Coleridge & White Ltd, 20 Powis Mews, London W11 1JN.

69. Faber and Faber Ltd for 'Modern Love' from *Selected Poems* by Douglas Dunn.

70. 'Did This Happen to Your Mother? Did Your Sister Throw Up a Lot?' from *Good Night Willie Lee, I'll See You in the Morning* by Alice Walker, published by The Women's Press. Reprinted by permission of David Higham Associates.

72, 79, 147. 'Deceptions', 'Toads' and 'Church Going' are reprinted from *The Less Deceived* by Philip Larkin by permission of The Marvell Press, England and Australia.

73. 'A Blade of Grass' from *Love Poems* by Brian Patten, published by George Allen and Unwin Ltd (1981). Copyright © Brian Patten 1981. Reproduced by permission of the author c/o Rogers, Coleridge & White Ltd, 20 Powis Mews, London W11 1JN.

77. 'A Martian Sends a Postcard Home' is from *The Onion, Memory* by Craig Raine. Reprinted by permission of the author.

85. Carcanet Press for 'Welsh Incident' from *Complete Poems* (1995) by Robert Graves.

97, 128, 156, 169. Faber and Faber Ltd for 'Follower', 'Mid-Term Break', 'Digging' and 'Blackberry-Picking' from *Opened Ground* by Seamus Heaney.

98, 103, 125. 'Timothy Winters', 'Ballad of the Bread Man' and 'I Saw a Jolly Hunter' from *Collected Poems* by Charles Causley, published by Macmillan. Reprinted by permission of David Higham Associates.

101, 176. The Society of Authors as the literary representative of the Estate of A.E. Housman for 'In Valleys Green and Still' and 'Into my Heart An Air That Kills'.

102. Shiel Land Associates for 'The Miner's Helmet' from *Collected Poems 1958–1982* by George MacBeth, published by Hutchinson.

111, 161. 'April Rise' and 'Christmas Landscape' from *Selected Poems* by Laurie Lee. Reprinted by permission of The Peters Fraser and Dunlop Group.

112. 'Peace in the Welsh Hills' by Vernon Watkins is reprinted by permission of Gwen Watkins. Copyright © Gwen Watkins.

114. Laurence Pollinger Ltd and the Estate of Frieda Lawrence Ravagli for 'Bavarian Gentians' from *The Complete Poems of D.H. Lawrence*.

115, 143. J.M. Dent for 'A Peasant' and 'The Bright Field' from *Collected Poems 1945–1990* by R.S. Thomas, published by J.M. Dent & Sons.

116, 118, 153. Faber and Faber Ltd for 'Wind', 'The Horses' and 'The Thought-Fox' from *The Hawk in the Rain* by Ted Hughes.

117. The Estate of Robert Frost for 'Stopping by Woods on a Snowy Evening' from *The Poetry of Robert Frost* edited by Edward Connery Lathem, published by Jonathan Cape.

120. The Society of Authors as the literary representative of the Estate of Laurence Binyon for 'The Burning of the Leaves'.

123. 'Let Me Die a Youngman's Death' from *The Mersey Sound* by Roger McGough. Reprinted by permission of The Peters Fraser and Dunlop Group on behalf of Roger McGough.

129, 138. 'The Death-Bed' and 'Base Details' by Siegfried Sassoon. Copyright Siegfried Sassoon by permission of George Sassoon.

132. Faber and Faber Ltd for 'View of a Pig' from *Lupercal* by Ted Hughes.

135. 'Long Distance II' is from *Selected Poems* by Tony Harrison. Copyright © Tony Harrison.

136. 'Death of a Son' from *Selected Poems* by Jon Silkin, published by Sinclair-Stevenson.

144. Seren for 'Sometimes' from *Selected Poems* by Sheenagh Pugh, published by Seren (1990).

150. 'Prayer' is from *Mean Time* by Carol Ann Duffy, published by Anvil Press Poetry (1933).

154. 'Dis Poetry' is from *City Psalms* by Benjamin Zephaniah, published by Bloodaxe Books. Copyright © Benjamin Zephaniah 1992.

158, 186. Faber and Faber Ltd for 'Little Gidding' (I) and T*he Waste Land* (*II. A Game of Chess*) from *Collected Poems 1909–1962* by T.S. Eliot.

160. A.P. Watt for 'The Rolling English Road' from *The Collected Poems of G.K. Chesterton.*

163. Faber and Faber Ltd for 'I think continually of those who were truly great' from *Collected Poems* by Stephen Spender.

172. 'A 14-Year-Old Convalescent Cat in the Winter' by Gavin Ewart. Reprinted by permission of Margo Ewart.

179. Faber and Faber Ltd for 'The Horses' from *Collected Poems 1921–1958* by Edwin Muir.

183. The Literary Trustees of Walter de la Mare, and the Society of Authors as their representative for 'The Listeners'.

185. 'Fifteen Million Plastic Bags' by Adrian Mitchell. Copyright © Adrian Mitchell. Available in *Heart on the Left: Poems 1953–1984* (Bloodaxe Books, 1997). Reprinted by permission of The Peters Fraser and Dunlop Group on behalf of Adrian Mitchell. Educational Health Warning! Adrian Mitchell asks that none of his poems are used in connection with any examinations whatsoever.

INDEX OF POETS' NAMES

— ◇ —

INDEX OF FIRST LINES

— ◇ —

Y

THE NATION'S FAVOURITE POEMS

ISBN: 0 563 38782 3

In a nationwide poll to discover Britain's favourite poem, Rudyard Kipling's 'If—' was voted number one.

This unique anthology brings together the results of the poll in a collection of the nation's 100 best-loved poems. Among the selection are popular classics such as Tennyson's 'The Lady of Shalott' and Wordsworth's 'The Daffodils' alongside contemporary poetry such as Allan Ahlberg's 'Please Mrs Butler' and Jenny Joseph's 'Warning'.

Also included is the poignant 'Do not Stand at my Grave and Weep'.

Also available:

The Nation's Favourite Poems
(hardback gift edition)
ISBN: 0 563 38487 5

The Nation's Favourite Poems
(audio cassette)
ISBN: 0 563 38987 7

The Nation's Favourite Poems
(C.D.)
ISBN: 0 563 38289 9

THE NATION'S FAVOURITE LOVE POEMS
ISBN: 0 563 38378 X

In this wonderful selection of 100 favourite poems, poets from every age celebrate that most universal of themes: love.

As well as traditional lover's favourites such as Shakespeare's 'Shall I compare thee to a summer's day?' and Marvell's 'To his coy mistress', there are more contemporary voices such as Wendy Cope and John Fuller. The collection also includes the ten most popular poems from the recent nationwide poll – romantic classics such as Elizabeth Barrett Browning's 'How do I love thee?' and W.H. Auden's 'Stop all the clocks'.

An anthology that is as rich and passionate as the emotion itself, *The Nation's Favourite Love Poems* will meet all your romantic requirements.

Also available:

The Nation's Favourite Love Poems
(hardback gift edition)
ISBN: 0 563 38432 8

The Nation's Favourite Love Poems
(audio cassette)
ISBN: 0 563 38279 1

The Nation's Favourite Love Poems
(C.D.)
ISBN: 0 563 38284 8

THE NATION'S FAVOURITE COMIC POEMS
ISBN: 0 563 38451 4

This wonderful anthology contains some of the nation's all-time favourite comic verse. From much-loved classics such as Lewis Carroll's curious 'Jabberwocky' to lesser-known and forgotten gems such as Gelett Burgess' 'The Purple Cow', Griff Rhys Jones takes us on a poetic tour of the witty, the nonsensical and the plain laugh-out-loud funny.

The selection brings together poets from every age and every walk of life, from Shakespeare to Victoria Wood and from Keats to Benjamin Zephaniah. There is Roald Dahl's cunning variation on 'Little Red Riding Hood', Spike Milligan's brilliantly ridiculous 'On the Ning Nang Nong' as well as several entries from the ever-elusive Anon, including the delightfully succinct 'Peas'.

Remembered, half-remembered, cherished or written on a tea towel, here are some of the riches that add up to the nation's favourite comic poems.

Also available:

The Nation's Favourite Comic Poems
(audio cassettte)
ISBN: 0 563 55850 4

The Nation's Favourite Comic Poems
(C.D.)
ISBN: 0 563 55865 2

THE NATION'S FAVOURITE SHAKESPEARE
ISBN: 0 563 55142 9

Recently voted Man of the Millennium by BBC Radio 4 listeners, William Shakespeare is one of the most enduring and influential writers of all time. This delightful celebration of his work brings together over 100 best-loved speeches, scenes and sonnets, all of which are guaranteed to appeal both to seasoned Shakespeare enthusiasts and to the uninitiated alike.

Complete with scene-setting passages for every extract and a foreword by Richard Briers OBE, *The Nation's Favourite Shakespeare* is a unique treasure-trove of familiar and forgotten gems that you are sure to reach for again and again.

Available from October 1999:

The Nation's Favourite Shakespeare
(audio cassette)
ISBN: 0 563 55331 6

The Nation's Favourite Shakespeare
(C.D.)
ISBN: 0 563 55336 7